DOCTORS AND THE LAW:
DEFENDANTS AND
EXPERT WITNESSES

Doctors
AND THE
Law

DEFENDANTS AND
EXPERT WITNESSES

Hon. Hiller B. Zobel AND
Stephen N. Rous, M.D.

W. W. NORTON & COMPANY / NEW YORK / LONDON

The text of this book is composed in New Baskerville
with the display set in Bauer Bodoni Black Condensed.
Composition and manufacturing by
The Maple-Vail Book Manufacturing Group.
Book design by Beth Tondreau Design/Mary A. Wirth.

LIBRARY OF CONGRESS CATALOGING-IN-PUBLICATION DATA
Zobel, Hiller B.
Doctors and the law: defendants and expert witnesses / by Hiller B. Zobel and
Stephen N. Rous.
p. cm.
1. Medical personnel—Malpractice. I. Rous, Stephen N. (Stephen
Norman), 1931– . II. Title.
[DNLM: 1. Malpractice—United States. W 44 Z83d]
RA1056.5Z63 1993
346.7303′32—dc20
[347.306332]
DNLM/DLC
for Library of Congress 92–16344
ISBN 0-393-03450-X

W.W. Norton & Company, Inc., 500 Fifth Avenue, New York, N.Y. 10110
W.W. Norton & Company Ltd., 10 Coptic Street, London WC1A 1PU
1 2 3 4 5 6 7 8 9 0

For Donald S. Lamm, to salute a half-century of friendship.

Contents

PART TWO:
THE DOCTOR AS WITNESS

Introduction

Learned Hand, a great judge, once ranked participation in a lawsuit as only slightly less painful than serious illness. We agree. But because legal entanglements, like ill-health, can snare anyone, no matter how exemplary the character or blameless the personal and professional life, we have written this book to offer you, a suddenly distressed doctor, some help in a time of trouble. Our goal is not to help you win your case; that is your lawyer's job. Instead, we will give you some information that we hope will ease your adjustment to a totally new and often terrifying experience. If what we have to say also encourages anyone else involved in a lawsuit, on either side of the "versus," so much the better. Justice operates better when every participant knows what is happening, and why.

Start with the Rush of Doom. What up to now has visited only someone else—a colleague, a friend, or a classmate—has at last come right to your own door. For no discernibly valid or fair reason, the Law and, worse, the lawyers have reached grasping hands into your life, at best needlessly interfering

with your practice, at worst slandering you and threatening your license, even your property. Or so you think.

This disaster can adopt different scenarios, each of them traumatic:

- As you come in for an afternoon of office appointments, your receptionist tells you that a man dropped off an envelope, which she hands you. Inside, you find three pages of legal jargon, headed by the title of some court. This document features your capitalized name and the label "Defendant." Reading further, you see words like "negligence," "failure to meet accepted professional standards," and "damages." After the last, you see a dollar sign preceding seven figures (the last six of them zeros).

- You are home enjoying a rare uninterrupted evening with your family. The doorbell rings. A neatly dressed stranger hands you a piece of paper and some money. "That's the attendance fee, doc," he tells you, and strides down the driveway. In big letters the paper says: "SUBPOENA—You are hereby commanded to appear" at some court next Monday, just at the time when you normally scrub. This Missive from Hell closes with the comforting warning: "Hereof fail not, under penalty of law." It does not define "attendance fee."

- The morning's mail brings a letter from a law firm whose multipartner name you have never encountered before. "This office represents Arthur Schwach, a patient of yours," it starts. "On his behalf, we have commenced an action for damages against Paul Behrer, M.D. I understand that you treated my client for the injuries sustained thereby. I would very much like an opportunity to discuss this entire matter with you." At least the letter closes "Sincerely yours."

- Sometimes the lawyer's missive carries a more pointed and bothersome message. For example: "This office represents your patient, Gladys Canby, who, as you know, sustained serious multiple fractures and internal injuries in an automobile accident. We have commenced an action

in Superior Court against the person responsible, and would like to discuss the case with you. First, however, we would ask that you furnish us with a complete and up-to-date report on Ms. Canby's treatment, present condition, and prognosis."

- You take a call at the office from a lawyer friend who tells you she has a prospective client with what seems a pretty good claim against a local physician in your specialty. Would you, the attorney wonders, be willing to look at the record and give her your opinion? As it happens, the incompetence of this particular doctor has long stimulated scrub-room discussions and lamentations among his peers; the question of terminating his privileges is even now the subject of investigation by a committee which you chair.

From long experience, we know that whatever countenance the Law may affect when it first greets you, chances are good that you will not regard the encounter with anything but fear and loathing, even if the judicial system wants nothing more of you than your testimony or opinion. That reaction is both natural and understandable. Nothing anyone can say will make the prospect pleasant. Remember, though, much of your anxiety comes from uncertainty and ignorance about the process. Ignorance not merely about technicalities that lay people—which in this context includes you—instinctively attribute to the law and the courts; ignorance about what being an unwilling part of the legal process will mean to you.

Our treatment plan is simple. We will rely, and we will ask your reliance, on the same problem-solving methods and attitudes you have been using all your professional lifetime. Whether you are reading this book as a prospective defendant, as a first-time expert witness, or simply as an inquiring fellow professional wondering how to relate to lawyers, we aim to give you the confidence that knowledge imparts, so that you may deal confidently with what now seems to you, as it has to many others, a harsh and hostile environment.

To do that, we will accompany you through each step. We

will explain what you can expect; we will point out pitfalls; we will suggest some pointers on dealing with lawyers (whether they be your champions or your adversaries); we take you on a familiarization tour, right into court, even into the witness box. Throughout, we will demonstrate that even though you may not be totally in control of the situation, you have much more of a say than in the first shock you think you have.

In short, we offer neither a cure nor a placebo. Just honest, straightforward explanations and encouragement from a physician and a judge.

(A word about form and pronouns. Chapter by chapter, we will apply either the feminine or the masculine to *all* the dramatis personae: physician, patient, expert witness, and attorney. We hope this will be less confusing than random gender shifts.)

Acknowledgments

Although any errors or omissions are entirely the authors' responsibility, they would like to thank, for their careful and extensive criticism, Robert R. Carpenter, Esq.; Earle E. Crandall, M.D.; and Stuart A. Schlesinger, Esq.

Our editor, Hilary Hinzmann, gave us insightful and appropriately inciting guidance.

Margot W. Rous and Rya W. Zobel blessed us with the taste, judgment, and love which illuminated our work and in a real sense made it all possible.

PART ONE

The Doctor as Defendant

When the Law Collides
with You

When you, as a physician, think of the legal system, "philosophical" is probably not the word describing your frame of mind. "Homicidal" might be more accurate. "Lawyers, judges, I despise them all," a doctor tells us. This physician, who has never faced a malpractice claim and testifies without particular discomfort, explains her scorn. "All that the lawyers want—whether they're defending or attacking the doc—is to win, and to hell with the truth. Now I know that not all the complaints are phony; there are some people with 'M.D.' after the name who ought to be digging ditches instead of bungling stitches. That's not the point. The disgrace is that the method of neutralizing the incompetents seems to me to be geared first of all toward minimizing scientific accuracy and more important, toward maximizing the fee of *all* the lawyers, no matter whose side they're on. It's a damn lottery, and the judges are worse than the lawyers, because they let it go on."

For our friend, and for the medical profession generally, "contempt of court" precisely depicts the average physician's attitude.

If that is your honest feeling, you need not apologize. Emotion is by definition irrational. Recognizing one's emotion, however, does not automatically validate the assumptions which underlie the feeling. Still less does acknowledgment of emotions justify yielding to them. Getting angry at the law institutionally will help you deal with the legal system about as much as a patient's unfocused rage at illness speeds recovery. In fact, an angry doctor, in court or out, does not help herself, but gives the enemy considerable aid and comfort.

Even if at this point you implacably regard the whole legal system as your foe to the death, remember: In war, it usually pays to know your enemy. Here is where we invite you to a painless inoculation of philosophy.

In a society as complex as ours—indeed, in any society— the legal system serves only two purposes: regulation of conduct and resolution of disputes. Although this book will occasionally refer to the first purpose, it will focus almost entirely on the second.

A dispute is merely an intensified variant of the genus disagreements. The difference is that although a disagreement may remain unsettled—hanging in air, so to speak—a dispute usually carries with it the implied necessity of decision. You may well regard this as obvious, and it probably is. Nonetheless, the point bears emphasis, especially when considering your personal relation to and with the legal process.

A dispute achieves resolution in one of three ways: (1) One disputant gives up; that is, one party wholly accepts the other's view. (2) The parties work out an agreement. (3) Some person or institution outside the dispute imposes a solution.

Notice an essential difference between the last two possibilities. When the outside entity terminates the dispute, it does so without regard to the parties' assent. That, of course, is the difference between a settlement and a court trial. The outside solution, the trial, precisely because it is imposed, does not aim to make the parties content, other than by ensuring each a fair opportunity to present her side of the story. Instead of participant satisfaction, the dispute-resolution process, as the courts administer it, looks primarily to terminating the dis-

pute. A fair termination, preferably; but, above all, an end to the strife.

This produces two important consequences: Concluding the battle becomes a value in and of itself; and the process, accordingly, deals not with determining what the truth is (or, a cynic might suggest, where the truth lies), but, rather, with achieving a fair, an equitable, a *just* result.

Thus a lawsuit is neither a scientific inquiry, nor even an effort to determine all the facts, if indeed all the facts were ascertainable. As the late distinguished lawyer-ethicist Charles P. Curtis once wrote, the administration of justice is no more designed to elicit the truth than the scientific approach is designed to extract justice from the atom.

This is not to imply that, despite what our doctor friend said, the legal process cares nothing for the truth. During a trial, truth, in the sense of honest testimony, is vitally important; the criminal penalties for perjury underline this concern. But the Truth, as an ultimate explanation, is not.

Among other things, many questions that society wants trials to settle are not susceptible of a True answer. What, for example, is "reasonably careful"? What are a particular child's "best interests"? Was the criminal defendant "capable" of conforming her conduct to the requirements of the law?

The legal process seeks to bring before the judge and jury (the "trier of fact," or "factfinder") the best available honest evidence: truthful witnesses, untainted documents. It then asks the factfinder to consider the evidence and to answer a narrow question or set of questions. Sometimes the questions go to the jury in written, detailed form; sometimes the jury need only respond generally: "Guilty," "Not guilty," "We find for the plaintiff and assess damages at———dollars," "We find for the defendant."

The mind-set and method we have been describing probably leave you, a physician, a scientist, baffled and outraged. If the court makes a witness swear to tell "the truth, the whole truth, and nothing but the truth," how can it care so little for the ultimate truth? Moreover, if, as lawyers like to boast, a trial is the only way to get at the real truth of a matter, why

does the law so impede a witness who knows what she is talk-ing about—a doctor, for instance—from giving the jurors exactly the information they need? Beyond that, why are trials so conducted that, as even the great legal scholar James Brad-ley Thayer admitted, the characteristic of the courts' approach to evidence is the exclusion of data really likely to prove some-thing?

These frustrations are perfectly natural. They are symp-toms of your internalizing the single most unpleasant truth confronting any physician involved in malpractice litigation, whether as defendant or witness: You are not in control.

No one feels secure in a situation where someone else gives the orders, where someone else sets the psychological pace. A physician encountering the legal system undergoes a partic-ularly acute form of mental agony. Whatever your practice or specialty, you are used to having people come to you for advice and treatment. You are used to the patient's entrusting her-self and her loved ones to you, relying on your skill, your judgment, your ability to make good things happen and bad things disappear.

You are used to speaking in a special language, using pre-cise anatomical, pharmacological, and etiological terms you are somewhat proud to know, and that not everyone (least of all the average patient) understands. You are probably more than willing to convert the technical lingo into lay speech, but by doing so you are of course reinforcing your self-image as One Who Knows.

When you go to a court of law, that comfortable, normal relationship changes. Now *you* are the outsider, intelligent, yet uncomprehending, and therefore, like anyone else facing a new situation, tense and—let's admit it—frightened. "Being in court for me," wrote Dr. Robert Goldwyn in his memoir *Beyond Appearance,* "was like being in the hospital for a patient: neither of us would willingly choose the experience if we could get the result by other means." And he went on to capsulize his feelings: nakedness, shame, impotence, and discomfort.

Most people, physicians or not, in court for the first time, would probably experience the same syndrome, the anxiety-

of-the-uninitiated, even if the case concerned nothing more than the location of a side-yard boundary. When the issue is not a lot line but your professional reputation, and in a very real sense your life itself, the tension passes any normal stress limit.

How can you cope?

The answer is something you already know. How many times have you emphasized to a patient that recovery is a team effort, that you will be providing the professional advice and service, but that the patient's own attitude and will to get well are even more important?

Now, although someone else is the professional and you are taking the dependent's role, the principle is still valid. We are going to help you put it to work.

CHAPTER TWO

You and Your Lawyer

Although as a malpractice defendant you feel betrayed, hurt, threatened, vulnerable, and scared stiff, never forget that you are not facing the crisis alone. You will not be left suspended at the end of a chromium wire. An astute, skilled professional is and will be at your side. Of course, you will ordinarily not have any input into the selection process. The company that provides your malpractice coverage will retain (and pay) the attorney.

If you wish, you may *consult* any lawyer you choose; he, however, will not represent you in the lawsuit. Even if you were willing to pay the lawyer's fee out of your own pocket, the company would almost certainly not agree to the arrangement. The insurer reasons that, over the years, it has come to rely on particular lawyers and to feel confident in their professional ability; it does not want to risk *its* money—which, after all, is the company's stake in the outcome—with someone unknown. Unless your malpractice policy is unusual, it expressly gives the company absolute control over the selection of counsel.

Understandably, you may be less than enthusiastic at the prospect of entrusting your career, your financial and emotional security, your family's happiness, and everything else you hold dear, to an individual you have never met, assigned to you arbitrarily. Nor does your anxiety level moderate when you realize that the person who is supposed to represent your interests may well have gone to law school with your tormentor, and almost certainly regularly breaks bread with him at Bar Association meetings.

Nonetheless, a close, professional working relationship with "your" lawyer is essential if you are to pass through this time of trouble with a minimum of pain and scarring, both emotional and financial. Remember, patients brought to the emergency room, or coming "cold" to the clinic, also must rely on the skill and competence of a total stranger. We urge that, from the start, you consciously try to put yourself in tandem with your attorney.

Unfortunately, the relationship typically begins in tension and distrust. Having received a legal-looking document embellished with the name of some court and festooned with allegations that you have erred professionally, you have notified your insurance agent, or your carrier directly.

We will underline at this point the vital necessity of making sure that any legal document which comes to you (whether or not your lawyer sent it) receives immediate attention. Indeed, whenever you receive from any person or organization anything having to do with the malpractice claim, you should promptly telephone your lawyer to report the arrival. Then forward the original, keeping a photocopy for your own files.

Do not, under any circumstances, respond to the document's sender, even if the material comes from the court itself, or from some other official-looking source. Let your lawyer handle any necessary communications.

Beyond that, a firm bit of advice. Let your lawyer attend to *all* communications with *anyone.* This comes under the heading of reality acceptance. A word misstated can literally lose your case for you.

Of course you will be tempted, probably more than once,

to tell "that money-grubbing ex-patient and his not-much-above-the-basement lawyer" exactly what you think of them. Or perhaps, on the other hand, your natural feelings of concern and compassion for a patient, even an ungrateful one, may spur you to write him a casual "human" note, expressing regret, without accepting blame.

Unfortunately, either course may lead to disaster.

When the tell-them-what-they-are impulse strikes, remember that anger is to common sense what paint remover is to fine enamel. No one can speak intelligently through clenched teeth, or persuade while roaring.

At best, your verbal outburst or (if you have been really foolish) your paper-scorching prose will create an impression of intemperate arrogance and excessive self-assurance. In short, you will project as just the kind of doctor who, after missing a diagnosis or faltering during a difficult procedure, would blame the world for his own shortcomings. Even an inexperienced lawyer will know how to cook you for breakfast, lunch, and dinner.

Oddly enough, the kind-and-gentle approach serves you just as poorly. You think you are being decent. The opposing lawyer will take your letter, at the very least, for what it is: a conscious expression of regret. He will then, easily and without any trickery, convert your expression of sincere sympathy into an admission of momentary incompetence. (We are talking here about communication *during* litigation. Conversation immediately after the medical problem becomes manifest is another matter, which we will discuss later.)

Now, if what we have been saying sounds to you like an unnecessary and unfair restriction of your right to free speech, and if your motto is "Be oneself," consider this: Even if your malpractice-insurance policy does not explicitly forbid giving the enemy aid and comfort, any act on your part which makes your case harder to defend can allow the company to claim noncooperation and to disclaim coverage.

Preposterous! you say? Cannot happen! you insist? We think differently; but let's not quarrel. Put it this way: Legally and factually, it is possible. However, with a bare minimum of self-

control, you can absolutely guarantee that it will not happen. The choice is yours.

Up to this point, we have been talking about "your" lawyer. Of course, as professional relationships go, the tie between you and the attorney the insurance company has selected is just a marriage of convenience. You probably never even knew the attorney's name before receiving a phone call or letter notifying you of the appointment. If, as we suspect, you also share the widespread public distrust of lawyers, you may be heading for a first-class disaster.

Here is another example of the need to depersonalize your role as a defendant. The lawyer who has been thrust upon you looks for his fee to the insurance company which has been annually receiving your malpractice premiums. Without knowing anything about the company, you can probably be pretty sure it is not a charitable institution; nor is it likely to be noted for tenderness of heart toward plaintiffs or openness of purse toward their lawyers. One other fact ought to offer you some comfort as well. Dealing with a large number of malpractice claims has probably given the company much valuable experience in defending doctors. This all might plausibly encourage you to have as much confidence in the defense battery as, say, you would expect from that patient you treat in the emergency room who knows nothing about your skill and experience.

Nonetheless, as we have said, you are entitled to consult any lawyer of your choice. Indeed, if the claim is so large that a substantial chance exists that the plaintiff may recover an amount in excess of your policy limits, the company will almost certainly give you an opportunity to retain counsel to protect your uninsured interest. In the overwhelming majority of cases, however, that is not necessary.

One caution. If, for any reason, you retain your own legal adviser, make certain that he and you understand that your legal team can have only one captain: the insurer's designated lawyer. Resist any temptation to play off the attorneys against each other. And make certain that your counsel remains merely your adviser and does not, by word or act, interfere with your

defender's work. Back-seat driving is no more appropriate in the courtroom than in the operating room.

Please note, however, that we are in no way seeking to limit your right, actually your duty, to ask the company-appointed lawyer questions. Any malpractice lawyer, whichever side he normally represents, knows that (a) the most important part of the defense ensemble is the defendant; and (b) an informed defendant, who understands what is going on and his role in it, makes the most dangerous adversary. Doesn't that exactly describe how you want the plaintiff's lawyer to think of you?

Informing yourself by asking questions calls for intelligent, purposive interaction between you and your lawyer. How, where, and when contact takes place is something you will work out together. Your unfamiliarity with the legal system and your high anxiety level can work in your favor. The key, as in so much of professional life, is organization.

To minimize the demands on your time, and to maximize the value of conferences with your lawyer, get a loose-leaf notebook, the kind that has dividers. In one section, keep an agenda of matters you want to discuss at your next meeting with the attorney. In another, jot down facts about the case that from time to time pop into your memory. The mechanics of human recollection work idiosyncratically; little points come to mind for no apparent reason, and in no particular order. When a thought occurs to you, write it down. Do not try to evaluate the legal significance. Of course, some matters which you may consider absolutely central may turn out to be wholly irrelevant. On the other hand, something which you regard as marginal may strike your lawyer as useful, perhaps even vital.

Sometimes, perhaps often, the lawyer will disregard your suggestion. Do not let your understandable disappointment cut off the flow of your ideas. The lawyer's job requires him to assess facts unemotionally, relating them to the legal framework.

Recall with what distressing frequency patients develop fixed yet erroneous self-diagnoses or concoct homemade treatment plans, equally useless. In responding, do you not try to take a

middle ground, correcting the misapprehension, yet not constricting the full reporting of symptoms and self-observation?

Apply the concept to yourself. Relate to your lawyer exactly as you would have a patient relate to you: Be informative, and receptive to expert professional advice. That way, you will maximize your usefulness to the defense team, and thus to yourself.

Here is where the notebook plays such an important role. Use it, first of all, to record adventitious recollections and ideas. In another section, list technical publications that pertain to the medical subject of your case: references to textbook sections, for example, or an article you see or learn about. If you think the printed material particularly significant, insert a photocopy right into the notebook.

One section should contain everything that you remember about conversations (both before and after the treatment) with the patient (and, in the case of a child, the parents), the adult patient's family, and *all* professional colleagues—not merely physicians. Be as full and specific as you can: who was present; what everyone said; where the conversation took place; how long it lasted.

You will need a section in which to keep any notes you make of your conferences with your attorney. And, finally, use a section to file any copies of court papers which your attorney gives you. We are thinking here particularly about formal questions, called interrogatories, a subject to which we will return a little later.

Now all this may seem an excessive demand on your time. Naturally enough, you resent any moment that the lawsuit steals from patient treatment and life-living. Yet although you may not at first realize it, the notebook will minimize the time and attention you must give up; more important, it will concentrate your energy and your thought, and thus will maximize the value of the hours and energy you perforce devote to the case. Beyond that, by merely performing useful work, you will find yourself feeling better about what is happening, because you will be asserting a measure of control over an otherwise overwhelmingly hostile situation.

In crises, most people tend to wring hands; a few ring bells. We invite you, for your own sake, to join the minority. Perhaps the best argument for the notebook is that many tough, experienced trial lawyers use this very device to prepare for trial. Why not give yourself the same advantage?

CHAPTER THREE

A Suit Is Not a Shroud

et's talk frankly about a subject that causes doctors to write some of the most vilifying prose this side of group defamation: the contingent fee, that arrangement between lawyer and client which makes the lawyer's compensation totally outcome-dependent. Eliminate this obscenity, one distinguished obstetrician recently thundered, and "malpractice claims would plummet with immediate and dramatic relief of the current crisis."

No one can dispute that America is an overlawyered society, with a penchant for litigation. Still, malpractice claims do not depend on the contingent fee; they arise because some patient believes that a doctor has rendered substandard care. So long as the patient, for whatever reason, maintains high expectations, and so long as carelessness exists (as of course it does, in medicine as in every profession), society will have to provide a compensation system. We can tell you, from personal observation and from frank discussions with hundreds of doctors, that medical people sometimes err seriously.

However, even if we had a no-fault, no-lawyer arrangement, some institution would have to identify the valid claims and work out fair payments. Of course, the funds would have to come from somewhere, most probably either by universal direct contribution (read, taxes), or indirectly, through payments by doctors (read, liability-insurance premiums), passed on to the patient (read, doctor bills or costlier health-care insurance). Further, unless one postulates a system in which no one, patient or physician, is allowed representation, and *everyone* must appear on her own, lawyers will necessarily become part of the process.

Perhaps here, as elsewhere in life, the devil you know is no worse than the devil you don't. The contingent fee remains in the legal system not only because lawyers are content with it, but, more important, because the public desires it (including doctors injured in auto accidents or suing to recover for bad investment advice). Moreover, the good news is that the uncertain nature of the recompense, combined with the high percentage of verdicts for doctors, encourages lawyers to select cases very carefully.

We stress a fact not often appreciated by anyone other than judges and malpractice professionals. When malpractice actions actually go to trial, the doctor wins nearly 80 percent of the time; in some states, even more often.

That's right: You read correctly. Despite all the angry talk about what the distinguished obstetrician calls "the wild and sweeping escalation" of "the malpractice litigation ripoff"; and notwithstanding the jolt your own insurance premium gives you, the plain truth is that when plaintiffs have to face the jury, only one in five takes anything home.

No one is really sure why this should be so. Some attribute the trend to the screening system that most states have established to make sure that any prospective malpractice action persuades a judge or a panel (including at least one health-care professional) that the allegations rest on something more than an attorney's hopes. This explanation, however, does not make much sense. If the panels sift out the cases resting on thin evidence of medical fault, the remainder should, by def-

inition, contain only those cases which demonstrate solidly (or at least relatively palpably) that the doctor miscued to some significant degree.

Other students of the phenomenon think it flows from an educational advertising campaign which the malpractice insurers sponsored in the early 1980s. Although the ads did not saturate the media, and in fact may have passed unnoticed by a large swatch of the population, the theory is popular among lawyers who usually represent plaintiffs. A contrary school, however, interprets the statistics as reflecting increasing public sophistication, and a growing realization that no physician can ever have a perfect record, because sometimes, to paraphrase a former best-seller's title, bad things do happen to good people.

Beyond this, the truth is that most Americans think pretty well of doctors as a group. Compare the way those occasional profession-popularity polls rate physicians with, say, lawyers. In all sections of the population, one finds a vast reservoir of good will toward doctors. So pervasive is this favorable feeling that, frankly, most of the time the lawsuit is for the doctor to lose, not for the plaintiff to win. In short, rather than raging against the system, particularly if the facts do not support your intuition, concentrate your thought and energy on intelligently working out an effective solution to your own immediate litigational crisis.

Successful litigation strategy and psychology depend on persistent application of a principle that has been bred into every first-year medical student for generations: *Primum non nocere* (first do no harm).

The old saw means just as much in a lawyer's office and court as it does in an examination room and hospital. Whatever you do, don't make things worse.

This brings us back to something we have mentioned before: your need to deal with the frustrations that result from your inability to control events and from your conviction that disaster lies just over the horizon. Like most of us facing a situation in which someone else is pulling the strings, you tend to respond with the devil's emotions, fear and anger.

As to the first of these, a lot of what FDR reminded Depression-ridden America in 1933 pertains just as acutely to your own present-day depression. And, as you have already come to understand, much of your fear proceeds from your never before having had to face the business end of a malpractice claim and the concomitant judicial proceedings. Here, as elsewhere, increasing familiarity will reduce the psychological dislocation.

At any rate, after the initial jolt, fear will most likely sound only in the background of your emotions. Anger, by contrast, will be right at the front of your consciousness, occasionally erupting in a froth of bile and fury when specific litigatory events provoke it.

The first of these will probably occur when you learn that the plaintiff's attorney has not plucked the allegations against you from a cesspool, but actually has in hand a written opinion by a licensed physician saying: (a) your conduct did not meet accepted professional standards; and (b) your failure to measure up caused your patient harm.

When you see a copy of this document—as you surely will—your reactions will probably follow a predictable path: first, incredulity that any sane individual, physician or not, could fault your performance; next, contempt for the jerk who would let herself be used (or who would, for a few dollars, prostitute herself into a hired gun); and, finally, dismay at the betrayal by a member of your own profession.

The coda to this crescendo is almost invariably a blast of rage that momentarily takes you right out of your mind. Under the circumstances, fury, irrational and inaccurately based though it may be, is only natural. Giving vent to it is in many ways healthy. But the trick is to make sure that whatever your feelings, and however vigorously (or even violently) you express them privately, you never do so in public. Beyond that, your emotions must never cloud your judgment or deflect your understanding of the steps necessary for maximizing your chance of ultimate triumph. In the world of malpractice litigation, keeping cool is the best revenge.

Unfortunately, under present-day circumstances the facts

of court life operate against you. Cases come to trial, and hence to resolution, only slowly (sometimes very slowly), typically, after two to three years—or more. You will daily wish that the whole dreadful business were behind you, and your impatience will goad your already strained psyche beyond what you may ever have imagined you would have to face.

Worse, because days and months will go by without the end appearing any closer, or (as far as you can tell) without anything happening, you, like most healthy people, may react by pushing the matter almost out of your thinking. Indeed, you may well be tempted to hope, and even to believe, that your former patient has come to her senses, appreciated just how hard you were trying to help her recover, and consequently called the whole thing off.

Don't you wish!

Depend on it: The day you telephone your lawyer to find out if maybe, perhaps, possibly, the case has died—that will be the day the lawyer says: "I'm glad you called. I've just heard from the other side, and we're going to have to. . ."

False armistice. The war continues.

The first battlefield—that is, the first place you personally will have a chance to observe a piece of the fighting—will probably be a lawyer's office, when you show up for your deposition, a necessary unpleasantness we'll discuss shortly. In some states, however, before a plaintiff can go much beyond merely commencing the lawsuit, she must demonstrate that her claim rests on something more than hope.

Typically, the lawyer prepares a documentary presentation built around medical records and featuring a written appraisal of your performance signed by a physician. The material comes before a screening body of the type we mentioned earlier. Sometimes the "panel" is just a judge; more likely it includes two additional members: a doctor and an attorney.

This procedure, instituted in the late 1970s at the insistence of the medical profession and the malpractice insurers, seeks to eliminate the kind of quick-hit claims which were bedeviling medical practitioners. In general, although doctors understandably do not think the review is nearly strict enough,

the process has worked reasonably well, and is widely credited with playing a significant role in reducing the flood of malpractice suits.

Unfortunately, statistics give little solace to a physician facing the agony of maligned professional competence. In addition, two aspects of the screening process are likely to cause special emotional difficulty.

To begin with, American society has long nurtured the idea that presenting one's claim for adjudication is a fundamental right. So deeply held is this concept that it has passed into the language; everyone uses it, even in contexts far removed from litigation: "A day in court," meaning "a chance to persuade."

Echoing this tradition, judges generally dislike cutting off a claim before the claimant can at least get into the batter's box, even if she will almost certainly never reach first base. The courts have therefore construed the requirements so as to establish a very low threshold of probable success. Essentially, to survive the initial pruning, a plaintiff need only produce a letter from a physician expressing the writer's opinion that the defendant, failing to meet acceptable medical norms, injured the patient.

This mild standard produces the second root of your unhappy reaction to the screening procedure. Treatment, whether medical or surgical, is both an art and an inexact science. Many times, even in those cases which clearly suggest a treatment of choice, reasonable, skilled practitioners can and do differ. After all, what else are second opinions for?

Given this less-than-micrometric precision, it would be a superhuman doctor who did not take serious umbrage at the thin evaluation which suffices to provoke the ordeal. In most cases, you will never have heard of the opining physician, and she will never have seen any part of your patient except her hospital records.

Add to that the acute feeling of resentment which will sweep over you at your betrayal by this unknown member of your own profession, who may, in fact, not even belong to your specialty. This last is the bitterest pill of all. In many states, so

long as an individual holds a medical degree and license, the courts will receive her opinion, even on questions far removed from her particular area of practice (in both the medical and geographical senses).

Our only advice at this point: Try to accept what seems so unfair as just another of the indecencies with which the malpractice suit is afflicting you; try not to lose your sense of perspective. And, above all, remember this: The opining physician usually finds pontificating by mail much easier than testifying in court. Dictation entails no risk of cross-examination.

On the Firing Line

For you, the lawsuit which the ex-patient (or the ex-patient's family) has launched is at best unnecessary pain, at worst unmitigated torture, and each procedural step is nothing but harassment.

If, however, you would—for present purposes only—consider things through the eyes of an objective onlooker, you might notice that the legal proceeding's ultimate aim is neither sadistic nor destructive. It is simply to do justice between the parties. Put another way, the judicial system, as we have suggested earlier, seeks to bring the dispute to a fair termination.

Understandably, you equate a "fair result" with the plaintiff's total surrender. The plaintiff, of course defines fairness as payment rivaling a 10,000-to-1 Kentucky Derby payoff. But that mythical individual the Average Citizen, strongly seconded by his equally imaginary cousin the Unbiased Observer, views a fair result more objectively, specifically, as answers to a series of questions:

What, in fact, was the physician's conduct?

Did that conduct fail to meet ordinary medical standards?

If so, did or did not the doctor's behavior inflict bodily injury on the patient?

What amount of money will properly compensate the plaintiff for his pain, suffering, and financial losses?

As it happens, the tests which the law applies pretty much follow the ideas of Average Citizen and Unbiased Observer. At the trial (if the case goes to trial), the judge will therefore tell the jury to consider the evidence in light of those tests. More important from your standpoint, whether or not the matter ever actually comes into a courtroom, the lawyers on both sides will constantly apply this legal litmus to the factual aspects of the dispute.

Each attorney necessarily keeps those principles firmly in mind as he goes about the business of gathering and assaying evidence. Every procedural step thus serves to measure your professional performance not in terms of, say, peer evaluation, but, rather, in relation to the standards the law imposes.

This difference in approach, invoking a quantum difference in method, attitude, and philosophy, frustrates and angers doctors. One example will suffice. A physician might say, "I was honestly trying to do my level best for the patient. Things didn't work out as I had hoped and expected. But I thought and still think that the treatment I ordered was going to lead to an improvement in the patient's condition. Isn't that enough?"

The legal answer is, No. What the doctor thought or believed is significant; but his good faith does not end the inquiry. If a physician, with the best will in the world, acts in a manner inconsistent with the professional behavior to be expected of the average practitioner in the doctor's specialty under the circumstances confronting him, the purity of the physician's motives will not alone exonerate him.

A doctor who lost a malpractice action wrote the judge afterward, complaining, among other things, of the judge's having "defined negligence as carelessness." Besides, he continued, "I have been taking care of patients as a staff physician for over 20 years. None has complained about my personal

care, my decision, or my physician-patient interactions." Maybe so. But a lifetime of careful performance is no guarantee that *this* time the doctor was not, at least in the jury's opinion, careless.

The law looks at the occasion involving the plaintiff; it ignores the rest of your life. If at that point you made the first mistake in fifty years of practice, you are, legally speaking, negligent. Prior perfection does not counterbalance the error.

One of the most important things you can do for yourself in the opening stages of legal confrontation is to accept these concepts. If that in turn leads you to grow comfortable with them, so much the better: Whatever you may think, they will govern your fate.

The lawyers will spend a great deal of time—much of it, unfortunately, your time—preparing for trial. Their modus operandi will probably strike you as something between inefficient and absurd. Watching a lawyer "work up" a case will probably strike you as the exact opposite of the way you approach a medical problem.

You take a history, conduct an examination, and obtain (usually fairly promptly) the results of one or more laboratory tests or specialized investigative procedures. Then, relying on your training, experience, and judgment, you determine a course of treatment and proceed to administer it, after conferring with the patient and obtaining his informed consent when necessary. In short, your way of doing things is to gather the needed data and to deal with the identified problem as quickly as possible.

Observing an attorney in action, however, you see a professional method that appears to work something like this:

The conclusion—that is, the professional's goal—is laid out from the start. Depending upon which side of the "versus" his client occupies, the lawyer wants either to maximize or to minimize the plaintiff's recovery. He then seeks information to buttress this preselected (or, if you like, preordained) position. Whereas a doctor looks for facts in order to reach a conclusion, a trial lawyer looks to the desired conclusion to determine what facts he needs to seek.

Of course, in neither instance is the pattern so clear-cut. A physician, for example, often comes very quickly to a tentative determination of the medical answer and then proceeds, as he acquires more and more scientific evidence, to "rule out" possible alternative answers. And a lawyer, although setting out to achieve his client's goal, sometimes finds, as the legal and factual research advances, that the law or the facts (or both) simply will not support the client's aim. However, unlike the physician, who must treat the patient for whatever ailment the data disclose, a lawyer who comes to realize that the client's cause rests on an untenable basis must cease pressing it, or defending it, as the case may be.

At the same time, the lawyer has a firm professional obligation not to abandon a client merely because the going seems rough and success uncertain. For one thing, as Dr. Johnson reminded Boswell, a lawyer must sometimes, for the benefit of the client, submerge his own doubts. This famous dialogue, too long to quote verbatim here, explains, from the nonlawyer's standpoint, a moral aspect of the legal profession that many lay people, including—perhaps we should say especially—many physicians, find both inexplicable and, well, immoral.

Boswell expressed discomfort at having to argue a position he knew to be bad. Johnson gave a three-pronged answer which when paraphrased is still valid today: First, the jury, not the lawyer, decides the merit of a case; second, facts that do not persuade the lawyer may nonetheless convince the jury; finally, the lawyer is not to judge, but to say all he can for his client, and then let the jury render the verdict.

Whether you find this reasoning personally attractive depends, of course, on whose lawyer's behavior you are evaluating. Philosophers call this the Gored Ox Principle. An attitude that you may quite understandably consider crooked shysterism in your adversary's attorney may draw plaudits as tough, honest representation when adopted by your own forensic champion.

This moral parallax (and paradox) permeates the judicial system, starting with the first exposure to that forced factual

striptease which the law calls "discovery," the process of gathering information for use at trial.

Discovery is one of those euphemisms which infect every profession. Lawyers swear at it, even as they practice it. Indeed, the word "abuse" seems as associated with "discovery" as the malaria virus with the anopheles mosquito. Yet the concept rests on a simple and unexceptionable principle: If all the parties to a lawsuit know everything pertinent to the issues in dispute, then (a) the trial will be more focused, hence shorter and thus more likely to produce a just, fair result; and (b) the probability of a settlement before trial will increase geometrically.

To maximize information-collection, the rules of every judicial system in the country permit a variety of court-regulated investigative procedures. You are almost certain to face three of these: one (documentary disclosure) you will regard as merely inconvenient; another (interrogatories), mildly intrusive; and the third (the deposition), entirely outrageous and meriting the separate-chapter treatment we shall give it.

As before, however, when we take you through the discovery process, we will, while acknowledging your feelings, accentuate the positive and, in explaining how each device operates, seek to address your concerns and to suggest the means for turning the ordeal to your own advantage.

Let's start, then, with what in health-care litigation is usually the gentlest form of discovery, a request for documents. The other side will want to examine every piece of paper (including photographs and X-ray plates) in your possession or control that pertains to the issues in dispute. This means not only documents in your office or home, but also those which may be physically in someone else's hands, but over which you retain possessory rights.

If, for example, you have given your attorney your entire correspondence file, he, acting in your behalf, will have to disgorge all pertinent letters. The measure of pertinence here is simple: Are the document's contents reasonably calculated to lead the other side to evidence (documentary or otherwise) that would be admissible at a trial?

On the other hand, correspondence between you and your lawyer discussing this lawsuit is ordinarily exempt from exposure, as are any notes or materials (written or oral) which your attorney may have generated about the current litigation. The contents of the notebook we have recommended that you keep are not *per se* subject to discovery; on the other hand, you cannot, merely by putting it in your notebook, shield material which is otherwise discoverable.

Now you can see why we classify document discovery as simply inconvenient. Indeed, if your office records are in order, complying with a show-us request merely requires assembling the papers and giving them to your attorney, who will check through the file to make sure it contains only material to which the opponent is entitled, and then will deliver copies (usually) to the other side.

A word of caution here: Leave the sifting and evaluating to the lawyer. Do not hold anything back, no matter how sure you are that it is neither important nor disclosable. And do not take this opportunity to improve—or, indeed, to change—anything in the file. Although the temptation may be strong to ensure that "the record gives the true picture," resist it vigorously.

Nothing "croaks" a case more effectively than evidence of document altering, document destruction, document backdating, or any other kind of document hanky-panky. The disclosure almost always comes during cross-examination of the physician, and leaves him vainly seeking instant invisibility while the jurors' scowls foreshadow a disastrous verdict.

This does not mean that you should not carefully *examine* each document before turning it over to your lawyer. You should. Nor does it mean that if you feel that a particular item is either incorrect or damaging you should not bring the matter immediately to your attorney's attention. By all means, do that as well. Here, as elsewhere in litigation and life, the onset of potential difficulty invokes the principle first enunciated by and named for the late Yale football coach Herman Hickman: If they're going to run you out of town on a rail, be sure to lead the parade.

The second common discovery device goes by a pompous title, interrogatories, but is nothing more than a set of written questions seeking discoverable information. Here again, the definition of "discoverable" encompasses any information that may reasonably promote the unearthing of courtroom-admissible evidence.

From a lawyer's viewpoint, interrogatories offer a cheap, simple means of learning essential facts. The attorney prepares the questions (or copies them from a form he has used in numerous earlier cases) and sends them to his opponent. He, in turn, reviews them with his client; obtains the information necessary for drafting the answers; puts the material in final form—i.e., in a manner calculated to minimize the information imparted, while maximizing "squirming room"; reviews them again with the client; and has him sign the final product, either under oath or immediately beneath an equivalent written antiperjury inoculant.

As you can imagine, interrogatories afford an excellent means of obtaining data: the names of the people in the operating room; the dates of the patient's treatment; the exact period the plaintiff stayed out of work; the amount of the plaintiff's lost wages. When it comes to narrative information, however, interrogatories fail badly. Consider a common case, far removed from the medical-care field.

The interrogatory: "Beginning at a point in time thirty seconds before the collision, and ending two minutes thereafter, please describe your actions in full detail, including, but not limited to, what you did, saw, felt, and heard."

The answer: "The defendant's car was speeding across the intersection so fast that I could not avoid him. The cars collided and I was thrown against the steering wheel. The next thing I remember was waking up in the ambulance."

Compare this scrawny response with what you would expect to receive if you asked the question in a face-to-face meeting. Not only would you anticipate a fuller answer right off the bat, but you would be able to follow up with another question—indeed, a whole series of questions, until you got the facts you were looking for.

Despite their obvious shortcomings to a lawyer trawling for useful information, interrogatories can, like bits of glass improvidently swallowed, wreak considerable damage. Remember, not only will you have to sign the answers, but you will do so under the same legal and moral compulsion that applies when you testify orally. Thus you would do well, as you sign, to imagine that you have just sworn that the document contains "the truth, the whole truth, and nothing but the truth."

Always remember that the opposing lawyer will read your words carefully, and with malice aforethought. An inaccuracy or an exaggeration will come flying back at you during cross-examination. Why hand your opponent ammunition? Instead, follow some simple, commonsense principles.

First, when you go over the interrogatories with your lawyer, do not try to ameliorate what you may think to be unhelpful information; do not hold back; do not edit. What the lawyer does not know, particularly if the ignorance is your doing, can and will hurt you. Lay out everything at all connected to the question, and let your lawyer put it into final form. At the risk of re-emphasizing the obvious, we remind you: For your own sake, never, never, under any circumstances, prevaricate, fake, or fudge. The doctor who would lie to counsel is at par with the patient who would give the physician a false history.

Finally, when counsel's finished product is before you, ready for signing, take the time and trouble to read it carefully. If something is unclear, ask for clarification. If something seems wrong, raise the issue firmly.

In short, although answering interrogatories does not normally rate as proactive forensic strategy, if you want to help your lawyer, make sure that your answers at least will not detonate against you when the fighting gets serious in the courtroom or in that preliminary ambush, the deposition, an exercise in litigational push-and-shove to which we will devote the next chapter.

Deposition: The Undress Rehearsal

A deposition is not the only discovery device, but it certainly runs far ahead of whatever may be in second place. No lawyer would ever permit a case to go very far without questioning the opposing party under oath. For reasons which you will immediately understand, the deposition permits counsel a matchless opportunity to learn, among other things: (1) what facts the other side knows; (2) what kind of appearance and impression she makes; (3) how persuasive a witness she is; (4) how vulnerable (or impervious) to cross-examination she is; and, not least, (5) how well she can stand the gaffe, take the heat, and generally control emotions and judgment.

Some physicians enjoy depositions; you probably will not. Even so, you can make this exercise, like many unpleasant-at-first-glance aspects of litigation, operate to your profit. The difference between agony and advantage is, once again, preparation. If you go into the deposition ready—psychologically, intellectually, professionally, and emotionally—the deposition, although no day at the beach, will offer you nothing more than transitory discomfort.

The deposition procedure is simple, but likely to accentuate your uneasiness. It can take place in a lawyer's office, although some attorneys prefer the physician-deponent's office, because the records are more readily available. Some defense counsel, however, resist that setting, because it affords the plaintiff's lawyer an opportunity to see what texts the doctor keeps handy, and may reveal other useful information.

Whatever the venue, the deposition will begin at a time agreeable to both attorneys and, believe it or not, with considerable regard for your schedule. Normally, you will have ample notice and plenty of input. Although no one encourages the dodge-and-weave tango, you will not have to reschedule your office / hospital obligations or your vacation.

Before the appointed day, your attorney will thoroughly discuss with you all aspects of the deposition that she expects the other side will cover. She will review troublesome parts of the case, and will probably have some ideas on how you can put your best foot forward. She may well suggest the lines of inquiry, or even specific questions to anticipate, without, however, telling you what to say. Apart from the obvious impropriety of coaching testimony, the forensic fact is that a witness who tries to follow a script generally blows the lines. Or, as the wise federal Judge Bailey Aldrich once wrote, calling upon his wide courtroom experience at the bar and on the bench, "Too many rehearsals can take the bloom off opening night."

This does not mean, however, that once the deposition starts you will be naked to your enemies. Your lawyer will be right at the table with you; and *she* will be counting on *your* help.

Do not expect to see your patient at the deposition (nor, if death has intervened, a surviving relative). The dramatis personae usually include only the two attorneys, the reporter (i.e., official stenographer), and the star of the show, you.

The proceedings open with the two lawyers, like opposing managers before a baseball game, going over the ground rules. What their palaver normally boils down to is an agreement that nobody gives up the right to object to a question later on unless the objection concerns form—i.e., wording. You will probably hear one of the lawyers intone, "Usual stipulation,"

or, somewhat more formally, "It is agreed and stipulated that all objections except as to form are reserved to the time of trial."

The stipulation at most forces the lawyers to pay close attention to the questions. When the structure of a question is proper but the substance is objectionable, the attorney loses nothing by remaining silent. Thus, for example, failure to object to a question eliciting hearsay ("What did the nurse tell you?") can be, as the lawyers say, cured at trial. On the other hand, silently allowing a leading question (where the interrogator puts words into the witness's mouth) usually waives any future remedy.

After these preliminaries, the reporter will address you in a fast-paced monotone: "Please-raise-your-right-hand-do-you-solemnly-swear-or-affirm-that-the-testimony-you-are-about-to-give-will-be-the-truth-the-whole-truth-and-nothing-but-the-truth-so-help-you-God-you-may-be-seated." However formulaic and full of symbolic abracadabra this little ritual may appear, remember that it puts you under specific legal obligations. Even though no judge is present, a deposition is an official court proceeding; knowingly making a false, material (i.e., significant) statement in a deposition while under oath or on affirmation constitutes the felony of perjury.

Following the oath / affirmation, the plaintiff's lawyer begins questioning. Deposition-taking, like surgery, is both an art and a science, so no description can fairly cover every attorney's technique. It is fair to say, however, that a reasonably competent lawyer will set out to achieve certain specific goals. At a minimum these will include: (1) committing you to a single version of the pertinent events, so as to preclude ambush at trial; (2) learning as much as possible about the facts of this particular case; (3) learning as much as possible about your professional and (within limits) personal background; and (4) getting an idea about your testimonial strengths and weaknesses. In many ways, this last is the most important, because, although the attorney can obtain factual information through documents, hospital records, and written interrogatories, only by the live confrontation at deposition will the lawyer be able

to judge what kind of an impression you are likely to make in court.

Knowing what the lawyer is after will probably make you feel more comfortable about the procedure. Do not let that knowledge tempt you into trying active countermeasures. If you resist the interrogation too vigorously, or if you try to outsmart the lawyer, you will probably find yourself very soon up a dark creek without any means of propulsion. Like many of the points we will be discussing in connection with the deposition, this principle will apply just as much to your courtroom testimony. Thus, in a real sense, the deposition gives you an opportunity to get yourself into shape for what is still to come. It is best, of course, not to make mistakes at any time. Better for you, however, to make them at deposition than in the witness box.

When it comes to giving evidence, the rules are simple:

1. Make sure you understand the question. Beware of double negatives ("Isn't it true, Doctor, that you didn't . . . ?"). Beware of double questions ("You heard her answer; you were speaking to her, weren't you?"). Beware of sandbag questions ("Have you stopped using recreational drugs?"). Beware of words or phrases with which you lack familiarity. This is not the time to affect knowledge you do not possess. If you want the question put in plain language, say so; politely, of course, but firmly. Remember, though, verbal clarity is a reciprocal obligation—a point to which we will shortly return.

2. Don't stall. It is appropriate, even mandatory, to make certain you know just what your questioner is asking. But it is not necessary that you figure out exactly why she is asking that particular question, or what she intends to do with a specific piece of information. And it is always risky to feign confusion simply to gain a little maneuvering room.

3. Answer the question. In other words, be sure to respond to the inquiry *and* to make your response only as long as adequacy requires. Each of these precepts carries equal

importance. No matter how silly or offensive the question may seem, if you understand it and it permits an answer, respond specifically. Conversely, once you have answered the question, shut up and wait for the next question. In practice, this demands considerable self-discipline. Suppose, for example, the attorney asks, "It's true, isn't it, that, when my client asked you whether the operation was dangerous, you told her that she was perfectly safe?" If in fact you told the patient that the operation was common and that complications, although possible, were rare, your answer to *the question as asked* should be simply "No." Resist the temptation (in this example) to "set the record straight." Wait for the question that asks, "What did you say to the patient about the risks involved?" Naturally you want to tell your side of the story; and you will certainly get the chance. But not while the other side is taking *your* deposition.

4. Obey your lawyer. If she says, "Don't answer that question," stop talking. If, while you are talking, she interrupts you with, "You have answered the question," clamp your mandible. If she says, "You may answer," do so. But beware if, after the kind of inter-attorney squabbling that depositions seem to foster, the *other* lawyer says, "Go ahead and answer." Remember, no matter how low-key, polite, and charming, that attorney is the Enemy. So don't automatically start talking. Instead, give your lawyer an inquiring glance; and hold your tongue until you get a green light.

5. Never argue with your lawyer during the deposition, or ask questions like "Why can't I answer that?" A deposition is not Grand Rounds; leave the educational improvements for later, more private moments.

6. Don't rush your answers. Just as stalling merely to ease the pressure can create difficulty, similar hazards arise from responding too promptly. Sometimes, a question which you consider harmless enough trips a warning alarm in your lawyer's trained mind. If you answer before she can interpose, the harm is done, and the damaging information, which may well not be subject to discovery,

is irretrievably compromised. In court, with the jury eagerly listening, this can trigger disaster. Even in a deposition, the blurting out can effect major trouble. So foster the habit of, first, letting the interrogator finish the question and, second, waiting long enough to allow your attorney to speak out. Even though, in the deposition context, objections do not have their normal in-court force, at the very least the interruption can give you a short mental breather. In fact, an alert attorney, if she observes that the client is under interrogative heavy shelling, can effect a brief *de facto* truce, to the client's great benefit.

7. Don't call time out too often. During your deposition, in contrast to the actual trial, you can, if you feel the need, interrupt the proceedings to consult your attorney privately. Use the privilege sparingly, if at all. It is definitely a bad habit to acquire, and can make you look like either a puppet, unable to move unless someone else jerks the strings; a dunce, so stupid that you cannot understand simple questioning; a rascal, plotting with the shyster at every turn; or a coward, afraid to tell the truth. Even though, as we have indicated, no one but the attorneys, the plaintiff, and the reporter is likely to be present, a competent lawyer will make good use of your behavior. She might, for example, put the matter to you thus: "Now, Doctor, I just asked you why you decided not to order an EKG, and before answering that simple question, you had a little powwow with your lawyer for—by my watch—almost two minutes. Have you got it straight now? Are you ready to answer?" Unless you have spent considerable time as a witness, an episode of this type will, at a minimum, so disconcert you that you may well sputter an answer that will cause serious damage at trial.

8. Assume that *everything* you say in the enemy's presence is being recorded. A deposition is not *Candid Camera;* yet many a witness finds, to her later chagrin, that words uttered during what she took to be a break in the action gave the opposition both aid and comfort. The antidote

is simple: Except for "Hello," "Goodbye," *"Gesundheit,"* and "Which way is the washroom?" do not speak until spoken to. And *à propos* washrooms, reception areas, and elevators: Be careful; a casual remark can find its way back to the other side. Lawyers do not normally bug their office suites or staff their buildings with retired CIA types. Still, a little discretion can never hurt you.

9. Keep in mind the uses to which lawyers put deposition transcripts. The transcript is the typed version of the reporter's record. You would be well advised to understand its significance. Obviously, the other side reads the transcript to learn useful facts—that is the transcript's *discovery* aspect. A second and equally common use is *evidentiary*. Plaintiff's counsel can introduce into evidence against you any part of your deposition. The fact of *your* having said it makes virtually any relevant utterance admissible at trial; statements by a *party* are not considered hearsay. Finally, the deposition transcript is a potent *impeachment* device. "Impeachment" here has nothing to do with expelling the President from office. As we will discuss with you in fuller detail later on, to impeach a witness—actually, to impeach a witness's credibility—means to introduce evidence encouraging the jury to disbelieve the witness. A statement in the deposition transcript that contradicts something you say at trial will come flying back across the courtroom at you, accompanied by something like: "Now, Doctor, you remember when we conducted your deposition, and you swore the same oath you just took here, to tell the whole truth? And you remember I asked you [quoting from the transcript] and you answered [quoting again], and that's different from what you told this jury a few minutes ago, isn't it, Doctor? So I'll ask you, which of your two versions is true?" Spoken harshly or gently, those words sting. All we need to say now is: Be aware.

10. Tell the truth, because the truth doesn't go without saying.

Millions for Defense

I t is a fact of litigation life that, considering civil cases of all kinds, not merely malpractice claims, out of every hundred commenced (i.e., actually filed in court), only four "go to verdict." Put another way, 96 percent of all lawsuits reach some kind of voluntary resolution short of a full-scale trial. Although this statistic varies a little from state to state, it stands up fairly uniformly across the nation. So, whether the lawsuit started in San Diego or in Savannah, whether it involves a mortgage foreclosure, an automobile collision, or an alleged misdiagnosis, the odds are 24-1 that the parties will cut their own deal, rather than take pot luck from twelve strangers.

Cases, including actions alleging medical malpractice, settle short of trial for one big reason: uncertainty. Right now, however, the important thing to consider is not settlement's metaphysics but, rather, the mere fact of its pervasiveness. You see, whenever a malpractice case ends by agreement, the *quid pro quo* is very simple: The plaintiff gives up the lawsuit; the defendant pays an agreed sum of money. An outside observer would probably regard the process as logical and almost ban-

ally unexceptionable. After all, most people accept certain truisms: Every story has two sides; there is some good in the worst of us and some bad in the best of us; peace is generally better than war; sullen certainty is preferable to anxious doubt.

Settlement of even a palpably ill-founded claim often makes financial good sense. Defending any lawsuit necessarily entails time and money. From every standpoint, therefore, is it not smart to pay a reasonable sum in order to limit costs, guarantee against a *conceivable* disaster, and end the distraction endemic to litigation, so that the doctor can move on to more important concerns?

When, as happens more often than physicians like to think, the claim instead has considerable merit, raising a real question as to the doctor's performance, and with considerable evidence of heavy resultant damages, the argument for a voluntary solution is even stronger.

In the case of a "thin" claim, both the disinterested observer and the cynic propose treating the entire matter as nothing more than a business proposition. They suggest evaluating the situation in cost-benefit terms, trying to decide whether the probable result justifies the expenditure necessary to achieve it. Lawyers, of course, have a phrase for this calculus: "costs of suit." That is the term a disinterested legal observer uses. A cynic, on the other hand, might say "nuisance value."

The inability to adopt a dispassionate attitude toward settlement varies directly with the adopter's immediate involvement—and logarithmically with his lack of litigational experience. When the outcome will affect someone personally, and when he has not been in court very often (if at all), he will almost certainly find himself totally unable to maximize rationality, or even to attain it. This is the psychological fact which spawned the maxim "Be your own lawyer, have a fool for a client." The concept that emotional distance lends wisdom is not, however, unique to the legal profession. Physicians, after all, do not minister to themselves, or even to family members.

Short of a criminal prosecution, no legal procedure so ignites the emotions of a defending party as an action alleging med-

ical (or surgical) malpractice. When a physician regards the patient's claim as medically unfounded, the plaintiff's lawyer's position as avaricious and dishonest, and the doctor's own professional honor—nay, his very essence—as unfairly put to hazard, the ability to weigh the evidence and to calculate the odds of success are, to say the least, severely hampered. In fact, the doctor probably cannot even begin to consider the possibility, let alone the advantages, of settling, of actually paying money to the ex-patient and the lawyer.

Most first-time medical defendants respond negatively and profanely to the initial suggestion of settlement. The most common term they use is "blackmail." Our cynical observer would probably say that any litigant finds it easier to adopt intransigence when the cost comes out of someone else's pocket, and that a doctor has little incentive to quit when he knows that, if fighting continues, the insurer will be underwriting not only the sinews of war but any unexpected (and, in the doctor's view, impossible) adverse result. Oddly, the insurers afford this attitude considerable tolerance. Many policies give the physician final say as to settlement.

The companies have also learned that the doctor's natural aversion to settlement may rest on an intuitive understanding of jurors' minds. A plaintiff-recovery rate in the 20-percent range suggests, even compels, the conclusion that, although it may seem to many physicians that the profession can barely breast a sea of malpractice claims, the average citizen (at least when serving in a jury) only infrequently condemns physician behavior. Bolstered by the statistics, the malpractice underwriters are more and more declining to settle, if the only reason for settling is institutional pressure to "move" a case. Instead, they retain expert consultants to review each claim and (most important) to assess it in a detached, cold-blooded way.

If the referral panel or screening physician concludes that the claim has medical merit, because the defendant-physician's conduct did not meet average professional standards and caused the plaintiff's injury, the company will make the plaintiff a settlement offer, factoring in both the extent of the

malpractice and the "exposure"—that is, the amount of *possible* and *probable* recovery. On the other hand, if the hard-boiled referees opine that the physician performed adequately (or that whatever the acts or omissions, they did not harm the patient), the insurer will not pay a dime voluntarily, even if in the course of pretrial or mid-trial discussions with the lawyers the judge himself urges settlement.

One case from our experience illustrates several of the points we have just been discussing. A young child had died of pulmonary complications, and the parents sued the doctor who, standing in for the child's regular pediatrician, had received their description of the symptoms during a brief telephone conversation. At trial, he said that he had told them he would see them at the emergency room if they wished to bring the child to the hospital. The parents, in opposition, testified that the doctor had said it was not necessary to go to the hospital. (This clash of recollections, incidentally, is quite common in *all* types of litigation.) At any rate, the child remained at home, and died the next morning.

Throughout the pretrial proceedings and right up to the close of the evidence, the insurer refused to make an offer. Then, although the defendant-doctor had proved himself a strong witness, the underwriters—while the jury was actually deliberating—re-evaluated the case and put $300,000 "on the table," which the plaintiffs spurned. Within an hour, the jury (who of course knew nothing of the negotiations) brought in what lawyers call "a defendant's verdict," completely exonerating the doctor, and giving the plaintiffs—and their attorney—exactly zero.

In another case, a neurosurgeon's scalpel had rendered the plaintiff a paraplegic. Halfway through trial, the insurer offered $1,200,000. Despite his lawyer's strong recommendation, the plaintiff opted to await the verdict. He got one, exactly $1,200,000 less than the offer.

Naturally, we also recall cases in which the plaintiff made a demand that, given the facts, seemed reasonable; yet the insurer or the doctor, or both, rejected settlement, only to

hear the foreperson announce an award substantially higher than the top settlement demand.

The operation of the jurors' decisional process is indeed unfathomable. Yet, although the jury system occasionally miscarries, and although it sometimes appears subject to emotive manipulation, it fills its designated role more than adequately. Remember, the questions we leave for jurors to determine are precisely those which generally do not admit of categorical or quantifiable answers. For example, what, after all, does "reasonable care under the circumstances" mean? And what is the correct dollar value of someone's pain and suffering? The necessary vagueness of the issues only magnifies the uncertainty inherent in *any* decisional process, be the decider judge, jury, or galloping dominoes.

Someone has said that although the most popular response in the world is "Yes," the runner-up is "No." As human beings, we all prefer knowing to doubting; we would rather get bad news than no news at all. The first great benefit which settlement confers is, therefore, certainty. Once a case settles, everyone knows the result. Whatever other emotions come into play—a matter we will take up shortly—at least anxious anticipation is not among them. Remember Justice Holmes' apt observation that "anxiety is what kills."

Even more important than knowing the outcome is understanding the finality that settlement brings. A jury verdict, after all, even a favorable one, does not necessarily end the legal battle. The loser may appeal. True, the verdict *qua* verdict is not something the appellate court can change; only errors of law by the judge justify reversal, not anything that the *jury* did. (Even if the appellate court concludes that the verdict represented a miscarriage of justice, normally all it can do is order a new trial; it cannot enter judgment for the defendant.)

However, in the American system of judicature, the law is ultimately what the higher courts (state and federal) say it is. This means that, although appellate judges profess to be, and generally are, result-neutral, they exercise largely limitless power in determining the final outcome of a particular case.

When reviewing the conduct of a completed trial, the upper court, as we have said, focuses on what the *judge* did or failed to do. Its chief areas of inquiry are the various rulings on objections to evidence, and the content of the judge's final instructions (or "charge") to the jury. The reviewing court first determines whether the judge committed *error*—that is, failed to follow a controlling rule of law. One common example is admitting hearsay evidence; another is omitting or misstating a legal principle in the course of charging the jury.

Now, the rules of evidence or of substantive law, although generally well understood, lack the precision of, say, the rules of poker, or even the infield-fly rule. Rational people can differ not only as to the meaning and import, but also as to the policy which any particular rule should embody. Thus, for instance, we generally do not permit Mrs. Early to tell the jury that two weeks ago she heard Nurse Cavell say that she saw Dr. Lightfoot close a wound over a visible retractor. Were Nurse Cavell in court, she could so testify, because she would be speaking under oath, in front of the jury, which could then form its own assessment of *Cavell's* credibility. When, however, Cavell's account comes filtered through Mrs. Early's recollection, we usually exclude it as hearsay: an out-of-court statement offered in evidence to establish the truth of its contents.

If courts adhered strictly to this rule, they would not be able to receive a great deal of evidence which a fair trial would absolutely require. Therefore, over the years, appellate judges have worked out a lengthy series of *exceptions* to the hearsay exclusion. For instance, a physician may testify to what the patient said about his subjective symptoms, or even about the way he sustained injury. The doctor may not, however, relay what the patient said *caused* the injury. Thus he may testify: "The patient told me he was struck by an automobile"; but he may not add, "He said, 'The driver ran a red light.' "

Opportunities for variant interpretation and carefully drawn distinctions thus abound. In many ways, predicting the result of any particular appeal can be as uncertain an exercise as jury-verdict prognostication.

Pass over the irritating fact that doctors (and scientists generally) find the law's indefinite certainties (or definite uncertainties) infuriating and frustrating. The important thing to realize is that whether a case "stands up" on appeal depends entirely on two basic determinations by the appellate court:

Did the trial judge misapply a rule or a principle?

If so, was the error merely "harmless," or was it "reversible"? That is, will the appellate court simply ignore the miscue, or will it upend the lower-court result entirely?

Although appellate judges insist that they decide appeals without regard to their views of the outcome "below," lawyers assume that the reverse-or-affirm issue turns on whether the appellate court likes the result of the trial. We bring this fact of life to your attention neither to provoke wrath nor to confirm prejudice, but merely to emphasize that uncertainty and lack of finality characterize every facet of litigation, *even after the jury has rendered its verdict.*

"I can call spirits from the vasty deep," boasts Glendower in Shakespeare's *Henry IV,* and Hotspur replies, "But will they come when you do call them?" Just so, when any elated litigant boasts after a jury verdict, "I've won!," the court-savvy observer always asks, "Yes, but will you keep the victory?" Without a settlement, no one can tell winner from loser. This is simply a practical application of Berra's Principle: It ain't over till it's over. Here: It ain't over because it ain't over, unless it settles.

Great though the value of certainty inherent in settling may be, the litigation's demise gives the parties an even more significant benefit: getting on with life, putting the litigation behind.

Whether the underlying dispute concerns professional competence, a defective appliance, a failed real-estate transaction, or a divorce, when the average person becomes involved in any kind of legal dispute, the dispute tends to dominate his life. Excepting masochists, lawsuit junkies, and those whose life motto is "Sue the Bastards!," most people, perhaps especially most physicians, put litigation low on the list of preferred quality-time activities.

Entirely apart from concern over the dicey outcome, the presence of a lawsuit in your life compels you to focus not only on the ongoing tactical and strategic issues, but also on the events of the past. A malpractice trial, like most litigation, seeks to re-create or recapture a series of bygone activities. In a sense, the trial is less drama than applied history, where people who *do* remember the past are, despite what Santayana may have said, nonetheless condemned to relive it. In a trial, remembering unpleasant matters becomes an inescapable duty. Even though a participant may wish desperately to let the unhappiness sink into oblivion, forgetting becomes not a virtue or a desideratum, but a deadly hazard.

Whatever may be the uses of history in a general sense, concentrating on one's own past experience, especially to the intense degree that litigation requires, does not make for health and happiness. The past's chief characteristic, after all, is its immutability.

Whether you regard your professional performance as proper or deficient, if you had it to do over, almost certainly you would have done *something* differently. Even if you are completely, absolutely, totally certain that no physician could have treated the patient better, the very presence of the lawsuit generates the unpleasant feeling of "If only I had [or hadn't] . . ." This desire to change the script does not limit itself to treatment issues. Unless you possess an ego larger than the Goodyear Blimp (a circumstance which carries its own problems, as we will be discussing later), you are almost sure to wonder whether you could have avoided all the trouble if you had been able to establish a closer personal relationship with the patient (or the family), either by taking more time to explain things, or by chatting, or just by saying something different.

The lessons you may have learned from the present imbroglio, however, will help you only in the future, not now. Intellectually, you fully understand and accept that fact. Emotionally, you will be less able to assimilate it. The constant tension between what you *know* and what you *feel*, between

reality and desire, between recognition of immutability and frustration at your inability to change anything, will seriously affect your entire personality. Added to the tension endemic to any litigant, and the special emotional stresses pressing a physician-defendant, the obsession with past events will depress and embitter you. Worse, it will deflect emotional, mental, psychic, and physical energy from your primary purpose, which is practicing your profession. Worst of all, everything bad about a malpractice affects your family just as much as it touches you—perhaps more.

In a very real sense, therefore, you need to bury the past and once again put your full thought and energy into treating your patients. Sure, you have been badly hurt. That, indeed, is the precise point we are emphasizing. Nothing will change the fact of the hurt; yet devoting yourself to *how* the hurt happened will not effect a cure. The incessant scab-picking which litigation demands will not aid the healing process. So long as the litigation dominates your attention, the process cannot even start.

Think on the patients you have known, going all the way back to medical school. Which generally were most likely to achieve maximum recovery in minimum time? Those who looked backward, or those looking forward? Those who literally lived in the unhappiness of the past, or those seeking consciously to do the best they could in the future?

Thus probably the greatest benefit that settlement confers is emancipation. When a case settles, it ends forever: no appeals, no new trials. Recollection becomes an entirely personal matter; now that the pressure to remember is off, you can at last let time, the ultimate cure, begin its work.

Does settlement present any downside risks? Like everything else in medicine and in life, it certainly does. First, the fact of the payout does go on your insurance record. Although one incident probably will not affect your premium rating, particularly if you never face another claim, the payment, as we have indicated, represents the insurer's judgment that you were indeed at fault, or at least that the evidence was strong

enough so that a jury would likely have found you so.

More significant, the insurer must report to the National Practitioner Data Bank *any* payment made on account of a malpractice claim based on a malpractice event occurring after September 1, 1990. The requirement applies not only when an insurer pays off a judgment after trial, but also when the payment results from a mid-trial settlement, a pretrial settlement, even the rare settlement occurring *before* the patient's lawyer has actually started court proceedings. Although claims against a hospital or a group practice as such do not trigger the obligation to report, the requirement does touch any individual physician working, say, for a hospital, if his actions generated a claim against his employer and a consequent payment.

In addition to the doctor's name, and the place and time of the offending conduct, the report must also contain the reasons for the claim and the manner in which and the date when the settlement occurred. The physician involved may obtain his own record, but not that of anyone else, although state boards regulating practice have access. When a doctor seeks hospital privileges, the hospital *must* check the NPDB file. Rest assured, however, that neither a prospective plaintiff nor an attorney can obtain the data.

Should the mandatory reporting affect your judgment about settlement? On the emotional level, the response has to be, How can it not? When you approach the issue, as you must, with logic and detachment, the answer is considerably less definite. Remember, your insurer must report *any* payment. Thus, whether the money passes after a six-week trial (and two appeals) or voluntarily, within a month after the lawyer's first letter, the Data Bank must learn about it.

We and you could engage in lengthy medicolegal dialectics, but the discussion would still boil down to this: What are the hard-nosed, realistic chances that a jury will return a plaintiff's verdict; and what is the likely dollar amount? Put another way, are the odds sufficiently favorable to justify your expecting a defendant's verdict? Betting on the outcome has this advantage: If you win, the Data Bank makes *no* entry. If you

lose, the jury writes the number; if you settle, you define the figure. Is it in your interest to decide just what the Data Bank will record? The question is not easy. The only consolation is that although you have nothing but a choice of evils, here, at least, you personally can exert some control over your fate.

CHAPTER SEVEN

The Anatomy Lesson

In that region of terror you find yourself crossing during the weeks before the actual trial, your sense of doom, like the anxiety that threatens your ability to function, grows out of one inescapable psychological truth: mankind's universal fear of the unknown. Knowledge and experience, of course, provide the surest analgesic; and of these, knowledge comes first, both temporally and in importance. That primacy has been, and will continue to be, the theme and aim of this book.

Resolving your concerns about the courtroom ordeal itself starts with a tour through the anatomy of a trial, just about the way your medical-school professors first introduced you to the intricacies of the human body. Remember how the anxieties vanished as your familiarity with the subject increased?

Many of the points we will be discussing here will come under further scrutiny later. The present purpose is to give you an overall view of a functioning lawsuit, leaving for future chapters a more detailed analysis of areas raising particular concerns. Some readers may find this rather basic. Our experience, however, suggests that even many law-sophisticated



48

doctors know less than they think they do about how courts actually run. (In this, frankly, they do not differ from that large majority of lawyers who deliberately structure their professional lives to pass as far from the courthouse as possible.)

Almost all malpractice trials depend for decision on a jury, most often twelve, sometimes as few as six ordinary citizens selected by lot and commanded to come to court. Formerly, "jury duty" required attendance for a period that could last a month or more. A "venire" (from the French for "to come," pronounced variously, "ven-*eye*-er" or "ven-*eye*-ree")—that is, a group of citizens called to jury service—furnished the jurors for all the trials occurring during that time, which meant that an individual juror might expect to sit on several trials. Because the service lasted so long, numerous professionals were exempted from any jury obligation, and juries tended to reflect not the public as a whole, but merely that portion of the population with time and inclination to enter the jury box.

Over the last dozen years, more and more states have abandoned the old system, turning instead to the concept of "one-day/one-trial" service. A citizen is committed to sit for only one day unless the trial lasts longer; if that happens, the juror must serve until the case finishes, at which point the obligation ends.

As a necessary and welcome concomitant to the reduced period of service, virtually all exemptions disappear. Everyone is eligible: doctors; lawyers; police officers; firefighters; clergy (a few years ago, the Cardinal Archbishop of Boston appeared for service, although his panel did not actually sit on a case); politicians; even judges (the Chief Justice of the Massachusetts Superior Court once sat—incognito to his fellow jurors—on a prosecution for murder). As a result, juries more fairly reflect the local population base.

The mechanics of actually selecting a case-specific jury vary. For one thing, although the great majority of jurisdictions still rely on the traditional twelve-person jury, some states, and some federal courts, use six-member juries. The actual selection procedure can also differ widely.

Many states, and all federal courts, permit very little ques-

tioning of prospective jurors, a procedure called "voire dire" (also from the French, "to see what they say," and pronounced "vwar deer" or "vwar *dye*-er"). Instead, the judge or the clerk briefly describes the case and puts a series of formal inquiries to the panel, questions like "Are you related to any of the parties or lawyers?" and "Have you formed an opinion about this case?"

Then, again depending on the local practice, the judge may allow the lawyers to suggest additional inquiries. Generally, however, in those jurisdictions which limit juror interrogation, the questioning does not dig very deep.

With open jury voir dire, the lawyers run the show; sometimes the judge is not even present. The lawyers may ask the prospective jurors directly about their experiences, their attitudes, and, indeed, about anything the attorneys may think pertinent to the way the jurors will finally vote on the verdict.

The object is to bring a person the lawyer does not wish as a juror to admit that she would not be able to decide the case impartially, and thus to receive an excuse "for cause." Although the exact number varies from state to state (and between states and the federal courts), each lawyer has only a limited number of chances (sometimes as few as four) to eject someone from the jury box without explaining why. From the days of John Adams, lawyers have always used their "peremptories" reluctantly. They would much rather not have to expend one, preferring to have the juror excused "for cause." No numerical limit applies to successful challenges of that sort. This results in a certain amount of pressure on the judge to define "cause" loosely.

The lawyers try to ask questions in such a way that the juror ultimately answers "No" to the inquiry "Well, in light of what you've been saying, do you really feel you could decide this case impartially?" An even better denouement comes direct from the juror ("I'm sorry, but I really do have a prejudice against doctors").

Lawyers have another reason to prefer letting ostensibly objectionable jurors in effect take themselves out of the box, rather than having to do it peremptorily. This scenario saves

the attorney from appearing to dislike or disfavor a particular person. She comes across instead as merely trying to make sure that the jury stands unbiased. That, at least, is the impression the lawyer hopes to create among those who will ultimately sit as jurors.

The primary purpose of voir dire, then, is the seating of an impartial jury—or at least a jury without any flagrant probable prejudices. A secondary aim, which our old friend the Cynical Observer might even consider its only aim, is to permit the attorneys a certain amount of preselling, an opportunity to begin the competition for the jurors' votes. Not surprisingly, jury selection can take hours, even days.

When the judge or clerk, rather than the attorneys, conducts the juror inquiry, the process certainly takes less time and, one must admit, reduces lawyer histrionics. Does this method produce a fairer or more balanced fact finder? Well, on that question the jury is still out.

Whatever the process, ultimately the jury box is filled, and then some. Whether with a traditional twelve-person jury, or a jury of six, one or two "alternates" also take their places, ready to fill in for any juror who for valid reason arising during the trial cannot continue to serve: a juror's sickness or death, death in a juror's family, or some similarly serious emergency.

Incidentally, although the government gives jurors a fee for their services, the amount is not even close to a reasonable day's pay. Many employers, although not all, reimburse the juror any difference between salary and the jury fee. This is not required; and if the juror is self-employed, daily income necessarily drops down to the daily pittance. For this reason, many unsalaried people ask for jury-service excuses, and the proportion of retiree-jurors is always high.

One other sidelight. We have occasionally referred to the federal court system. Malpractice litigation does not generally come there unless the patient (or, in case of death, the personal representative) and the doctor are citizens of different states. If *any* defendant shares citizenship with the plaintiff, the case *must* commence and remain in the state court. (If the

physician was a federal employee—a military physician, for example—the case is exclusively federal; but the only defendant is the United States. The doctor, by federal law, is not individually liable.)

Once the jury has been chosen and sworn, the judge will usually appoint one of the jurors foreperson. In some states, whoever occupies Seat Number 1 (or some other particular seat) gets the job automatically; sometimes the judge allows the jury to make its own designation. Whatever the method, selection as foreperson is not equivalent to nomination for Vice-President of the Universe. The foreperson presides over the deliberations, making sure that everyone has an opportunity to speak; tallies the vote; writes out any questions the jury may address to the judge during deliberations; signs the verdict slip; and announces the verdict or affirms it after the judge or clerk reads it aloud. The foreperson has no greater say, certainly no greater vote, than any other juror.

The trial itself begins with an opening statement by the plaintiff's lawyer. An opening statement is not evidence; nor is the lawyer supposed to argue, a guideline which does not always restrain zealous advocacy. Because even the best-run trials often have to accommodate to the out-of-court demands on witnesses' lives, and because in any event testimony does not always flow in logical sequence, jurors might have great difficulty following the evidence. The opening statement, by setting out the entire case, thus serves as a kind of road map indicating where the case is heading; or as the picture on a jigsaw puzzle box, showing where all the pieces fit.

After the plaintiff's attorney has finished, defendant's attorney may, if local practice permits and forensic strategy so dictates, make an opening statement as well. The lawyer generally asks the judge's leave, but unless the custom requires the defense to defer opening until after the plaintiff's evidence concludes, permission is never withheld. If the defense does not "open" immediately after the plaintiff does, the defendant's opening will precede the defense evidence, and thus may not occur until long after the start of the trial. Whenever it comes, the defense opening is likely to urge the

jurors not to make up their minds until they have heard *all* the testimony; less frequently, because lawyers consider surprise a major tactical weapon, counsel will hint at a few particular coming attractions.

When the lawyers have finished, the judge may give the jury a brief introduction to the applicable principles. (In some states, the judge does this *before* the plaintiff's opening.) The idea here is to let the jurors know exactly what the plaintiff is trying to prove, and the degree to which she must prove it. Not all judges "precharge" the jury; do not fear the worst if the judge remains silent and the next occurrence after opening statements is the arrival of the plaintiff's first witness.

Before anyone can testify, she must indicate, either by swearing an oath or affirming her intention, that she regards herself as *obliged* to speak "the truth, the whole truth, and nothing but the truth." The clerk customarily administers the oath or affirmation just before the witness enters the witness box. (The option of affirming is constitutionally protected in most states and the federal courts, to accommodate those whose religious principles prohibit oath-taking; the legal effect is the same.) Sometimes the judge herself conducts the ritual; sometimes the entire group of prospective witnesses takes the oath or gives the affirmation together, just before the trial starts.

However sworn, the witness "takes the stand." In some states, this literally describes the process: the witness remains on her feet throughout the interrogation. Most courtrooms, however, furnish a chair. The states also differ as to the lawyers' position while questioning. Most local practice requires standing upright; in some places, counsel remain seated.

The attorneys, not the judge, determine the order in which witnesses testify. More accurately, counsel's trial strategy sets the sequence. Conventional wisdom dictates that the evidence start and end with a "strong" witness, who will in one way or another favorably influence the jury. "This," as Illinois attorney Alan E. Morrill puts it, "is to make a favorable, strong first impression and then slam the lid down tight with the last witness."

The witness herself need not necessarily favor the side for whom she testifies. Indeed, as we will see, often the plaintiff's lawyer opens the testimony with the *defendant*. The thought here is plainly not that the witness will charm the jurors into finding for the plaintiff but, rather, that the evidence, dragged as it were through the doctor's clenched teeth, will by its own force sway the jury permanently.

After the lawyer offering—that is, calling—the witness finishes examination, the other side has the opportunity to cross-examine. Neither attorney may interrupt the other to question the witness; if a lawyer objects to a question or answer, she simply says, "Objection." This indicates more than that the lawyer wishes the question had remained unasked or unanswered. It means that she thinks the inquiry or the witness' statement violates some rule of evidence. The judge then decides one way or the other: "Sustained" or "Overruled."

If she has sustained the objection, the question remains unanswered, or the answer, if the witness has spoken it, goes "out." Of course, it not only remains in the transcript, but also to some extent stays in the jury's collective memory. It does not, however, form a part of the evidence on which the jury can properly rely when reaching a decision. Do the jurors forget something they have heard? Probably not entirely, any more than a judge would. Experience shows, however, that jurors take great pains to follow the judge's instructions, and that they do indeed disregard that which they are told to ignore. Even if they did not, we would probably have to assume that they did; otherwise, every time objectionable evidence reached the jury's ears, the judge would have to declare a mistrial and start the case all over. Instead, the judge tells the jury to ignore what the witness said, and the trial continues.

Following cross-examination, the original proponent may conduct redirect examination, usually limited to *new* matter brought out on cross-examination; judges do not like lawyers to hold for redirect what should have been brought out initially. After redirect, the opponent can re–cross-examine, similarly limiting inquiry to any new subjects raised during redirect. Again, this is not the time to slip in questions that

properly belong to the original cross-examination. No serious penalty attaches to re-covering old ground, although lawyers who habitually break the rule succeed only in exasperating judges; the slight evidentiary success rarely warrants the ill-will (which, by the nature of trials, the jury also acquires, and with amazing speed).

Sometimes local custom, or a tolerant judge, will permit a variant of the normal pattern: *re*-redirect examination, followed by *re*–re-cross-examination, and so on—up to the judge's estimate of the jury's patience, or the limit of her own.

Occasionally, the case involves more than the prototypical two parties (as, for example, when a patient has sued two doctors, or a surgeon and a nurse), or an original defendant brings in an additional party (as when the patient has sued the anesthesiologist and the hospital, and the hospital has claimed indemnity from the manufacturer of the ventilator that the patient says the personnel misused but which the hospital claims malfunctioned). In such a scenario, *every* party has a right to cross-examine, although common sense, a fear of boring or antagonizing the jury, and direction from the judge tend to counter the lawyers' inbred horror of leaving the last word unspoken.

At any point while examining or cross-examining a witness, counsel may wish to introduce what the legal profession, in unconscious irony, calls "real" or "demonstrative" evidence—that is, any physical object, as opposed to mere oral testimony or written documents. Thus an X-ray plate, a ribbon retractor, or a scalpel can come into the jury box, provided the item in court is the very one which played a part in the activity under consideration. The witness identifies the item, and counsel proffers it as an exhibit. Depending upon local practice, the clerk marks the object "Plaintiff's Exhibit 1" or "Defendant's Exhibit 1," or merely "Exhibit 1." In some courts, all of one side's exhibits carry numbers; the other's, letters.

Occasionally, although a particular witness will be able to identify an object generically, she will not have the firsthand knowledge necessary to tie it to the particular case. If, however, another witness will supply the missing testimonial link,

the object will be "marked for identification," normally with a letter ("Exhibit A for identification"), although here again local practice can vary. Marking an object "for identification" means that the item is not yet *in* the case, as a full-fledged exhibit. The procedure, however, avoids confusion. Instead of referring to "this scalpel," or "this object," or even simply "this," thereafter witness, lawyer, or judge having occasion to mention the item will call it "Exhibit A," thus ensuring that later on anyone reading the transcript will fully understand the speaker's reference.

If a witness simply wishes to use a particular object for teaching purposes, solely to make her testimony more intelligible, she may do so (although courtroom etiquette normally requires asking the judge's permission—which is almost always forthcoming). Counsel will then offer the item not as an exhibit, but as a rough diagram or what Massachusetts lawyers call a "chalk." Unlike an exhibit, this item is not evidence. Usually, it is a not-to-scale freehand sketch, which a witness draws on the courtroom blackboard or a large piece of paper, often to clarify spatial relationships.

The concept, however, has come to cover every kind of nonevidentiary physical item brought before the jurors' eyes (or even into their hands) which aids them in understanding testimony, including anatomy charts, skeletal models, and examples of pertinent medical instruments.

A variant of the chalk is the in-court demonstration. Here the witness brings materials to the stand and re-enacts for the jury what she would otherwise perform in the laboratory or the field. The show-and-tell can range from a simple chemical or mechanical run-through to a computerized video re-enactment. Again, whether or not the production goes forward depends on counsel's tactical decision, and in the end on the judge's discretion. As computer technology advances, we can probably expect considerable sophistication: a computer-drawn "replay" of surgery, for example; or even a "trip" along the alimentary canal or around the islets of Langerhans.

However mentally stimulating the exhibits, chalks, demonstrations, and reconstructions, they are not the central core of

the proceedings. For that, we come back to the testimony, the words the witnesses speak. A trial is an exercise in persuasion, but an exercise necessarily limited by the rules of procedure and evidence, by the materials available, and of course by the skill of the advocates. Whatever form the evidence takes, real-life litigation almost never matches the smoothness and excitement of a television or movie trial. This is not to say that drama, deliberate or unconscious, never enters a trial. It does, but not often; and even then, almost absent-mindedly.

Only during counsel's closing arguments does life begin to imitate art. Once both lawyers have finished introducing exhibits and examining the witnesses, the parties "rest," and the presentation of evidence "closes." Now overt advocacy commences.

Up to then, the advocates have directed themselves to the judge and the witnesses. Of course, any trial lawyer knows that nothing occurring in the jurors presence entirely escapes their notice. As an example, once a Boston attorney, talking to the jury after a lengthy, complicated, and losing effort, heard with astonishment that "we noticed you kept a heap of papers on your table—very disorganized. Gave us the impression your client was trying to hide something, or that you didn't know the real story."

Yet, despite the *given* of juror omnivision, and the attorneys' constant effort to shape their presentations to advance their clients' positions, the lawyers do not overtly *speak* to the jury until final, or closing, arguments.

Here again, the image exceeds the reality, and the living advocate often seems less genuine than the actor. Although many closings blend factual analysis and effective emotional appeal, most lawyers do not evoke images of Gregory Peck, Spencer Tracy, Susan Dey, or Veronica Hamel. Extemporaneous speaking always takes more effort than working from a script in short takes, with flattering camera angles, and plenty of time to get the whole thing just right. An actor-lawyer need only seem to make order out of chaos, winning the theater audience, not the actor-jurors she is ostensibly addressing. Her true audience, moreover, wishes to believe her and to accept

the scripted statements. A trial lawyer must convince real people that a flesh-and-blood client deserves to win, overcoming the listeners' doubts, perhaps even their hostile inclinations.

After the advocates have finished, the judge then "charges" the jurors, by instructing them in the legal rules they must apply when deciding the case. The court thus has the last word—except in Texas, where the judge addresses the jury *before* the lawyers do. Even in the more conventional courts, however, counsel have a pretty good idea what the charge will contain, because before final arguments (with the jury, of course, out of the courtroom), the judge has gone over with the lawyers what she intends to say. During that conference, the lawyers have the opportunity to request that the judge include (or exclude) particular language or legal phraseology in the instructions.

Bear in mind that the charge does not much concern the facts, because, just about everywhere in the United States, a judge may give her view of the facts only to a very limited extent, if at all. The lawyers therefore concentrate almost entirely on the applicable legal rules. Although many of these principles are well established, sometimes the evidence at a particular trial raises a legal issue that no case has yet brought up and that the appellate courts have not yet had occasion to consider.

Most cases do not produce any such "question of first impression." Instead, the lawyers ask the judge to state settled principles, thoroughly understood and accepted. Naturally, each attorney wants the rule enunciated in terms more favorable to her client. Whether the judge accepts a particular suggestion, she must let the lawyers know in advance, thus allowing them so to shape their closings as not to dispute what she will thereafter tell the jury. This deference flows directly from the almost universally applied rule that the law comes from only one source, the judge; jurors, individually or collectively, cannot decide the rules, cannot choose between competing legal principles.

Legally, and very often practically, the charge is the trial's most significant event, although the ordinary observer would

probably consider it at best boring. The legal importance is this: When the judge instructs the jurors about the applicable legal principles, she is in every sense laying down the law.

Suppose, for example, she says, "The plaintiff has the obligation of persuading you that the doctor did not tell her in advance about the risks of the proposed surgery." If, therefore, after considering all the evidence, the jury does not believe that the doctor failed to give the patient proper information, *the plaintiff loses*. If, on the other hand, the judge places the burden of persuasion on the defendant, telling the jurors that the doctor must convince them that she did adequately inform the patient, then it is the *doctor* whose evidence must sway the jury. If not, *the doctor loses*.

Well, you say, if the judge is not a free agent, able to follow her own idea of what the law is (or should be); if the judge may not properly allow her own view of the facts or the desirable result to affect the jury instructions; if the judge is bound by whatever rule the appellate courts have laid down; if all this is true, she ought to have no trouble determining the correct legal standard and explaining it to the jury.

Generally, she does not. Remember, however, that not all legal principles are clear-cut. Sometimes the state's supreme court has never established the particular rule; sometimes the rule, although previously firmly settled, is now in process of change.

Most of the legal rules governing the rights and duties of people to each other come not from legislation, but from decisions of appellate courts. This accretion of judge-enunciated rules is what we call the common law, as opposed to the statutory law. The mechanism permits the law to grow and change, gradually yet certainly, as it develops in response to society's emerging demands.

How does the common law transform an existing principle? Appellate courts modify existing principles, or make new ones, through revision of lower-court judges' work. They do not enunciate new principles or amend existing ones on their own. This is where the jury instructions play such a vital role. The principles change when an appellate court, reviewing what a

trial judge has said (or left unsaid), decides that although she spoke correctly, the rule itself must change. The higher court then states the new governing principle.

Note how this process differs from what happens when the higher court merely corrects a judge's misstatement of the law. Here we are assuming that the judge accurately and faithfully recited an existing rule, which the appellate court, for reasons of public policy, undertook to alter. Except for statutes enacted by the legislature, what we call "the law" is really only what the highest court in the state says it is.

This puts in clearer focus the relation between a trial and an appeal. The appellate court looks primarily at the lower-court judge's performance, not at the verdict. Although any one of the judge's in-trial decisions could, if the appellate court thinks she erred, result in a reversal, the judge's jury instructions provide the most fertile field for higher-court review.

After the judge finishes her instructions, the jury goes out to the jury room, deliberates, and decides the case. No one can listen in; no one other than the jurors themselves can be present. Nothing records the discussion. The various states set different proportions for a verdict. Some require unanimity; in others, nine jurors, or ten jurors, suffice. Occasionally, during their deliberations, the jurors wish clarification on one or another issue, usually some part of the judge's instructions. They write out their question and send it to the judge. She, in turn, discusses it with counsel, then has the jury brought back to the courtroom and gives them any needed further charge.

The jury takes as long as necessary to reach a verdict. In civil cases (as opposed to criminal trials), the judge almost never keeps the jurors overnight, sequestered at a hotel. Instead, if they have not concluded their business by the end of the working day, the judge instructs them not to talk about the case outside the jury room and sends them home until tomorrow.

In a civil case, only rarely does a jury ever report itself dead-locked, or "hung." The jurors talk until they have reached a consensus, and then they notify the judge, through the bailiff

or court officer, although they do not yet disclose the result. Judge and counsel resume their courtroom positions; the jury comes back into the jury box and then delivers its decision. Here again, local customs differ. In some places, the foreperson states the verdict; elsewhere, the court clerk or the judge reads the verdict from a paper, the "verdict form" or "verdict slip," which the foreperson has signed. Sometimes, losing counsel ask the judge to determine, by individual inquiry of the jurors, whether the court has received the verdict accurately; the decision to "poll the jury" depends entirely upon the judge's discretion.

At this point, one party has prevailed, although not necessarily "won" (the plaintiff may take a verdict awarding an amount lower than she anticipated—in some cases, lower even than what she could have settled for; sometimes, of course, the verdict is higher than the plaintiff's pre-trial figure). Although the other side may wish to appeal, neither dissatisfaction *per se* nor even the filing of an appeal leads automatically to a new trial. Unless the judge erred in admitting or excluding some particular item of evidence, oral or real, or unless she misstated the law to the jury, the verdict will stand. Put another way, no one can appeal a *jury's* decision. Only the *judge's* rulings or statements can come under a higher court's scrutiny. An exception does exist, to cover the off-the-wall, maverick, unsupported verdict. The definition of a legally intolerable verdict, however, goes considerably beyond the fulminations of a frustrated and unhappy defendant. We will explore this subject at greater length in a later chapter, and also the question of what a judge can do if she believes that, given the evidence the jurors heard, no rational jury could find for the plaintiff.

Suffice for the present to say that, although any verdict-loser can file and press an appeal, the success rate runs about one in six.

CHAPTER EIGHT

Into the Arena: The Bull's View

Today is the day—or, rather, the Day. However intensive the settlement talk between the lawyers, it has not brought results; or perhaps, despite your lawyer's advice (relaying the insurer's recommendation), you have for your own good reasons rejected the plaintiff's settlement proposal. So now you are coming onstage in the theater of your destiny. More likely than not, this is your first courtroom experience. *LA Law* and *Absence of Malice* don't count; nor do the times when, just to acquaint yourself with the scenery, you accompanied your lawyer while he argued one or another preliminary motion. A spectator is not a player. In adrenaline, sweat, tension, and embarrassment, watching a trial does not equal participating, much less filling the starring role.

Nonetheless, you would probably be wise to visit the courtroom once or twice during the week just before the scheduled trial date, even if you have been blessed (or cursed) with considerable prior in-court experience. Normal anxiety at facing new circumstances magnifies when the physical surroundings are also unknown territory. Scoping your mental sights will,

by the psychological effect of familiarization, help you to feel much less out of control. Besides that, if you happen to know the identity of the judge who will preside over your case, watching him in action may also reduce some of your new-kid nervousness. Better the devil you know than the one you don't.

Although basic procedures do not vary much among the states, or between your local court and the federal courts, a certain amount of difference does exist, even among judges sitting in the same building. Each presiding judge has his own set of idiosyncrasies.

Remember, whatever its purpose and ostensible format, a trial is above all a piece of theater. This is not to suggest that your trial takes place in a music hall rather than a hall of justice. Yet the two share so many attributes that anyone concerned in a trial who forgets the parallel can sustain irreparable self-inflicted damage. In a trial, the audience is the jury, unless the parties have unanimously waived their right to a jury trial; in that case—rare in malpractice litigation—the judge becomes a one-person audience. Never make the mistake of thinking that the spectators in the back of the courtroom are the audience. Those onlookers have nothing to do with the outcome. They are not like playgoers, capable of energizing the actors into histrionic superlatives. Nor are they like sports fans, inspiring the athletes to exceed prior limits. Ignore them.

Instead, train yourself to take the occasional fleeting look at the jury, as experienced lawyers do, to get some idea of how things are going. On the other hand, remember that jurors tend to believe that *their* role requires them to suppress emotion; they like to cultivate poker faces. Beyond that, sometimes one simply misreads the signs—experienced lawyers occasionally do *that,* too.

Like theatrical productions, trials also have actors, each playing a role: lawyers, parties, witnesses, judge. Moreover, the jurors, like any audience, carry unconscious role-expectations. Let one of the players deviate excessively from the pattern that the audience has, for whatever reason, assigned to that role, and the performer loses not only dramatic effec-

tiveness, but credibility and persuasiveness. If, therefore, the jury expects a doctor-defendant type to appear serious and concerned, a defendant risks disaster by constantly flashing a toothy grin, or conveying, through body language, an image of happy insouciance.

Again, an actor should wear a costume appropriate to the role. If in your community people expect professionals to dress conservatively, do not feel obliged to assert your personality by wearing a houndstooth sports jacket or a flowering cocktail dress. Although you may strongly believe that your clothing should make a personal statement, remember, the jury will make the final statement. You do not want it to begin: "We find for the plaintiff, and assess damages in the amount of . . ."

Another type of objectionable statement is electronic. Like most physicians, you probably carry a beeper. When you go to court, leave the little noisemaker home; if you feel you *must* have it with you, be sure it has been disabled. Some variant of Murphy's Law seems to afflict these devices during trials. They always sound off at the most inopportune times, like the crest of an escalating cross-examination, or the middle of the judge's jury charge. Just when the jurors' attention locks on the in-court event—*beep-beep-beep*. And there *you* are, frantically fumbling in your pocket or at your belt, looking and acting like a ten-thumbed fool, while jury and judge (and your own lawyer, if his was the performance your little toy interrupted) glower in annoyed frustration. Sorry. Your office and patients will just have to get along without you while you are on trial—or at least until you call in during the recess.

A play has scenery and props to help the actors create and maintain the dramatic mood that the particular plot requires. In the courtroom, the scenery is the room itself. Instead of props, the lawyers use photographs, X-ray plates, "chalks," surgical instruments, crutches, and wheelchairs. An imaginative lawyer can fashion an effective tool out of anything that (literally) comes to hand. One advocate, cross-examining the opponent's medical expert in a broken-leg case, effectively emphasized a question about the effect of trauma by suddenly and loudly fracturing the pencil he had been holding.

You will also notice that, like a good actor, a skillful trial lawyer will utilize the courtroom layout and furniture. The actor can, by body placement, take over the entire stage. A peregrinating lawyer, sidling up to the jury box or "charging" the necessarily immobile witness, can gain similar power over not only the room but the entire proceedings. Judges, however, also understand kinetic dynamics. To keep control, while yet avoiding a constant barrage of "Will you please stop moving around!" (which may itself suggest losing the reins), many judges simply install a small lectern, and require counsel to speak to jury or witness from there.

In a real sense, the trial of a case develops into a battle for control. This constant tension, so much like the conflict essential to any successful dramatic piece on stage, screen, or video, is exactly what attracts public interest and has inspired trial-oriented drama for centuries, from *The Merchant of Venice* to *The Verdict.* One of your lawyer's most important tasks will be to make sure that whatever part *you* play, the audience-jury will understand from the opening curtain that you are, if not the heroic protagonist, at least not the heavy or villain. Naturally, the plaintiff's lawyer will try to develop the opposite image.

The need for conflict and contrast prods both sides to develop a plot line that clearly differentiates good from evil. Unlike the many successful plays which achieve effect through emphasis of ambiguity, a well-lawyered trial never leaves the audience in doubt. From the first word of the opening statement to the emotional climax of the closing argument, a seasoned litigator stresses the justice of his client's cause, and thus, either explicitly or by strong implication, the opposition's iniquity.

Finally, just as every play—at least on its opening night— draws a reviewer, every trial carries a built-in critic. This one does not wear evening clothes, merely a robe. Here again, you will have to discard any recollection of the movie or theater stereotype. However sweetly good old Judge Weaver may have beamed on the combatants in *Anatomy of a Murder,* never forget that in a real courtroom the judge does not sit pas-

sively, speaking only when spoken to. Throughout all judicial systems, state and federal, the judge is the moderator of the trial, responsible for ensuring the orderly progress of evidence and witnesses and, indeed, the justice of the entire proceedings. Nor does one have to wait until the next day's papers to learn if this critic rates the production a hit or a flop.

Some malpractice trials rate a second critic: the insurance group's representative. He, too, will be rating the actors' performances; but his primary concern is prognostication, figuring out whether or not by the final curtain those performances are likely to have won the audience.

Now, although the theater-trial analogy can, like all valuable tools, exceed its usefulness, it teaches one especially worthwhile lesson. Never forget that, during every moment around the courthouse, you are in a real sense onstage. Whatever you do, someone will see; whatever you say, someone will hear. If you grimace, even briefly, while the plaintiff describes her injury, some juror will be sure to spot you, and will doubtless bring the episode to the panel's attention. It is, in fact, a truism among lawyers and judges that the jurors' collective eyesight is always 20/20: As a group they miss nothing.

Similarly, your casual remark in the courthouse elevator that, if you had it all to do over, you would have given the patient a much more careful explanation, will draw the attention of that harmless-looking fellow in the corner, who will turn out to be the plaintiff's best friend and will make sure that his lawyer gets the tidbit, in time to use the information at the point best calculated to maximize your disadvantage. As the posters warned during World War II, The Walls Have Ears.

If this all sounds like the counsel of neurosis, remember, the line between paranoia and precaution is not always sharp. Besides, even a paranoid can have real enemies.

The realization that you are always on public view can help in other ways. Depending on local custom, you may not be sitting at counsel table (another point in which life can diverge from the television). A spouse may quite properly accompany you and sit next to you in the spectator section. Your lawyer

will doubtless find some appropriate way to bring your joint presence to the jury's attention, as part of an entirely proper effort to humanize you and to make it easier for the jurors to identify with you as a person. At the same time, hand-holding, shoulder-gripping, or physical contact of any sort will immediately appear—to the jurors, the judge, and the opponent—as an attempt to influence the decision, an effort to win the jurors' sympathy. Your lawyer, seated facing away from you, will not have seen the display; the judge, however, certainly will. The least you can expect is a halt in the proceedings, followed by the judge's conferring with counsel, followed by your lawyer's conveying His Honor's firm instruction to cease and desist. If you continue, the judge may order your spouse to sit elsewhere, or else to leave the room entirely. In extreme cases, the judge may convey his views on decorum publicly, with the jury listening.

Similarly, you and your family (and friends) should understand that, although a trial is a dramatic event and an adversary proceeding, any physical, audible, or even purely facial display of emotional partisanship is entirely out of line. An expression of serious interest, but not a Great Stone Face, is the best course. Scowling in disapproval, head-shaking, nodding, sneering, and eye-rolling are examples of what to avoid. As for laughter, you will not err if you take your cue from the judge.

Judges tend to regard courtroom misbehavior personally, even if it does not amount to actual contempt of court. The judge is responsible, among other things, for the fair and orderly conduct of the trial. When spectator or party gets away with strange behavior, or even appears to do so, it reflects badly on His Honor. He will react accordingly.

Should you need to communicate with your lawyer, do it in writing, even if you are seated at counsel table. Generally, go easy on anything that the jury may interpret as sleeve-pulling or as an effort to take over the defense. What may seem to you nothing more than saving your lawyer from an avoidable mistake may appear to the jury as a no-confidence vote or, worse, an act of desperation. This is another of those pain-

fully frequent occasions in which you must live with being unable to control a situation that affects your career and your life.

By now, the anticipatory advice has probably seemed like Coming Attractions at the Spanish Inquisition. Your ordeal is going to end shortly, however, because the trial itself is about to begin.

First Blood—Yours

On the day your case is "called for trial," the parties and the lawyers appear in a courtroom where, after the clerk reads out the case's title, procedure follows the outline we covered in Chapter Seven. Once the jury has been seated and sworn in, the trial commences. The first event is always an opening statement by plaintiff's lawyer; defense counsel generally receives a like opportunity, although, for strategic reasons (or to conform with local practice), many lawyers prefer to reserve the opening until after plaintiff has "rested"—i.e., finished presenting testimony and exhibits. In either event, the operating rule is identical: An opening statement is not evidence; it merely offers the lawyer a chance to tell the jury how she expects the evidence will turn out.

Because an opening statement, particularly the plaintiff's, comes at the very beginning of the case, before the jury has heard or seen any evidence, judges usually insist that counsel omit all argument, eschew any overt attempt to win the jury, and instead concentrate on the expected evidence. That is a rule almost impossible to enforce.

Even an entirely correct, dispassionate recital of anticipated testimony can, by emphasis or mere placement of facts, argue passionately. A good opening seeks to begin persuading; and the best way to persuade is to suggest an air of impartiality. Remember Mark Antony's speech in *Julius Caesar,* which started off so mildly ("I come to bury Caesar, not to praise him"), and ended up rousing the mob against Caesar's killers.

Still, not every lawyer espouses subtlety. Many prefer the precept of the American Revolutionary Samuel Adams: "Put your enemy in the wrong and keep him there." Chances are, therefore, that you will have to endure an unflattering and inflammatory public denunciation of your deficient skills, your cavalier relation with the patient, and your inattention to medical details. Your natural tendency will be to jump up and remind the attorney of her canine ancestry and general unfamiliarity with the truth.

Resist the temptation. As we have suggested earlier, you will be more likely to help your cause by just sitting quietly, keeping to a minimum the grimaces, scowls, and unbelieving head-shakings. Remember, your time will come. Indeed, it may come with uncomfortable suddenness, because plaintiff's attorneys often call the defendant-physician as a witness *on behalf of the plaintiff.* Some even bring the doctor to the stand at the very beginning of the evidence.

It happens quite casually. The lawyer need give no advance notice, although of course you and your lawyer will have prepared for the call. Counsel simply announces, "Plaintiff calls Dr. [Your Name]." You proceed to the witness box, raise your right hand while the clerk administers the oath, sit down, and await the first question. You have now "taken the stand." As we have mentioned earlier, some states interpret the term literally, and the witness remains on her feet throughout the questioning. In most places, however, once you take the oath, you can expect to sit down.

The first thing to remember about testifying is that everything anyone says is literally "on the record." Whether the words come from lawyer, witness, or judge, all go into the court reporter's notes or tape recorder. Every aside, com-

ment, query, or inadvertent imprecation will find its way to immortality. Once the proceedings start, the phrase "off the record" means nothing unless the judge utters it, in which case the court reporter will stop memorializing the testimony. Although lawyers do not, at least in the courtroom, use the phrase with the aim of trapping you into making a self-damaging statement, whatever you say is, by its very nature, a public utterance. Judge or jury or both may hear it; opposing counsel almost certainly will. Guard your casual words as carefully as your formal ones.

As to vocalizing while on the stand, we tell you now what we will have occasion to repeat later: Say only what you must. Give the answer the question requires, nothing more. On the other hand, avoid silence when the inquiry plainly calls for an answer. An untoward diffidence risks this kind of thrust: "Well, doctor, that seems a simple enough question; any reason why you have taken half a minute to think up your answer?"

That last sally shows that the lawyer is aware, as you must be, that the court reporter—and through the reporter, the record itself—only notes what someone *says,* not what anyone *does.* Gestures do not appear in the record, nor unspecific measurements ("about this long"), nor vague locations ("in this part of the leg").

Those two facts—the record's unfailing retention of the spoken word, and its correlative total rejection of everything unspoken—combine to impose on you the vital necessity of remaining always alert. Like the lawyers, you must at all times "protect the record."

This is not to say that, unless something appears in the record, it lacks any significance. Far from it. Much of the most important part of the dramatic production we call a trial involves the effect on the jury-audience of evanescent matters which the court reporter completely and properly ignores.

To begin with, although your *testimony* is *what* you say, your *evidence* includes the *way* you say it. Is your voice level and controlled? Is it overly flat, arrogantly harsh, timidly inaudible? Are you testifying like a well-rehearsed automaton, or like an inarticulate airhead? And what about your hands? Are

you using them to talk? Do you clench your fists, as though repressing a desire to punch somebody? Are you constantly twining your fingers? When you speak, do you frequently put a hand in front of your mouth in a gesture some people interpret as an unconscious signal that you are keeping back the truth?

Don't forget facial expressions. Are you grimacing when you answer, thus creating the impression that getting facts from you is like pulling teeth? Does nervousness make you smile at inappropriate times? On the other hand, does your intensity make you excessively grim, so that, when your lawyer asks you to name your children (a common inquiry, aimed at encouraging the jurors to regard the defendant as an ordinary person, much like themselves), you resemble the FBI Director listing America's Most Wanted Criminals?

At this point, you may be wondering whether proper trial preparation requires a class in Method acting. If you are the sort who despairs easily, you may fear that the face and voice which have served you so well all your life will now become the agents of your professional doom.

These are natural enough feelings, but they miss the point. First, you need to understand, at all times, that testifying to a jury is quite different from, say, lecturing to students and residents during grand rounds, presenting an interesting case to a group of colleagues, or chatting with your office partner. Second, you must become aware of the kind of verbal and physical habits everyone has, habits which do not much affect your daily life, but which in a courtroom context can distract your listeners and divert their attention from what you are saying.

In short, you have to focus your mind, voice, and body, so that your message, your side of the case, and your personality all come through without interference.

Nothing anyone can say will ever make testifying a pleasant experience, especially for a physician defending her professional behavior. But if you learn to spot and avoid a few of the more common pitfalls, you can minimize the pain.

The guiding principle once again is the old medical standby, *primum non nocere.*

For a physician-party-witness (in fact, for *any* physician-witness, or indeed any witness at all), that boils down to one major precept: Understand what is going on. Make sure you are certain what the question seeks. If you don't grasp the lawyer's question, say so.

A word of caution here. If the question is plain, don't feign bafflement in an effort to gain time. You will only make yourself look tricky. The same thing goes for asking the lawyer to "repeat the question, please." That ploy will immediately cast you as sly, inattentive, or stupid, none of which is a personal adjective of choice. For the same reason, be careful of asking that the reporter "read the question back." Under no circumstances put the request to the reporter directly; the reporter works for the court, and takes orders only from the judge. Plop your foot into that relationship and you will be lucky to emerge with full ambulation after the judge, with the jury listening, sets you straight on courtroom protocol.

Lawyers make mistakes, too. Sometimes counsel, fancying herself an instant expert, will put a question so medically ludicrous that you will be tempted to offer an instant correction. Resist the temptation to lecture or laugh. Most jurors will identify with the layperson's ignorance, not the expert's smugness.

Fielding a hashed question on cross-examination, you can sometimes make points by rephrasing the garble and answering the revision. This raises serious dangers, however. Apart from the risk, once again, of coming across as a crafty smart-alec, you may inadvertently give the lawyer an unexpected gift, better for her purposes than the answer she expected. Your new material may be more useful to the other side than the original effort. Wisdom therefore suggests saying something like "I'm sorry, I can't answer the question the way you've put it." If the interrogator is your own lawyer, she will be grateful for a chance to regroup; if the opponent, she will at least not carry away anything valuable.

Be attuned always to the shape of the question, and deal calmly with any problem. You want to make sure of your ground, without conveying any hint of snobbery, slipperiness, or sarcasm.

- Look out for queries that carry one or more inaccurate assumptions, as, for example, "And after you reached the hospital at about ten, did you go directly to the patient?" (Suggested response: "I reached the hospital at eight-forty-five; then I went directly to the patient.")

- Be careful of the double question, especially when your answer to Part One does not cover your response to Part Two: "You really hadn't reached a diagnosis, and you had never met the patient before that day, isn't that so?" (Suggested response: "That's two questions in one; which should I answer?")

- Stay alert to double-negative questions (and double-aspect answers): "That doesn't mean you shouldn't perform the surgery, does it?" What does the answer "Yes" mean? Or the answer "No"? (Suggested response: "I'm sorry, I got lost in the double negatives.")

- Be wary of questions that invite you to say "No" when you mean "Yes," or vice versa: "In any event, you didn't observe swollen lymph nodes?" A "No" answer could be taken as short for "No, I didn't," or as a simple disagreement with the question. Similarly, a "Yes" could suggest either that you are really saying "Yes, I did," or that the questioner is correct. (Suggested responses: "That's correct. I did not"; or, "That's not correct. I did observe them.")

- And, of course, never fall for the bait of the question that cannot be fairly answered: "Have you stopped indiscriminately prescribing amphetamines?" (Suggested response: "I never have, and I don't now.")

Dealing with any of these darts is really just a matter of common sense and ordinary politeness. In fact, the best summary advice we can give comes not from the law or medicine,

but from a mother whose daughter was about to "go out" for the first time.

"How will I know what to do?" the youngster asked. "Well," the mother said, "sometime before your date arrives, open the refrigerator and take a look at the mayonnaise jar." Mystified, the daughter did what the mother suggested. On the label she read: "Keep cool, but do not freeze."

In your case, Doctor, we might add: Do not boil, either.

Taking Your Lumps— But Taking It Easy

Because no two trials are the same, no single scenario covers all. By and large, malpractice trials follow a common format. Thus, in your trial, the plaintiff's lawyer will probably call as the first witness either you or the patient (or, if the patient was a child or deceased, a parent or the surviving family member). A spouse, if the patient has one, will also testify, giving evidence of something called "loss of consortium"—that is, a derivative claim for lost companionship, service, society, and the like.

In many states, if the patient has children, they, too, are entitled to recover for lost consortium. However, unless they can add important particular details, youngsters do not usually take the stand. Some lawyers think it does not hurt to have the jury see them; most, however, believe the marginal gain more than offset by the strain testifying places on a child, and worry that the jury may in any event regard the maneuver as a blatant play for sympathy.

Whatever the order or manner of presentation, the testimony at this stage of the trial has two main objectives: to start

the jury thinking that you acted improperly; and to demonstrate the adverse impact that your mistake has had on the patient and the family. Unless the case involves a significant claim that you failed to inform the patient (or the parents) adequately about the risks involved in the proposed treatment, this phase of the trial will involve very little testimony about the purported malpractice. Instead, it will focus almost entirely on the patient's physical reaction (i.e., pain and suffering); loss of earning *capacity* (which may be an element of the case even if the plaintiff has never worked); and the effect of the medical result on the family.

Throughout this segment of the trial, you would do well not to dismiss the evidence as overplayed phony baloney, cooked up by a greedy, ungrateful ex-patient and an immoral, grubbing lawyer. Whatever may be the case's scientific or professional merits (or, as you would probably put it, *de*merits), even something fairly describable as "just an unfortunate medical result" can have genuinely horrendous effects on the patient and those close to him.

Your recognizing that fact will not hurt you or your cause. On the contrary, the more you can develop some degree of equanimity and detachment, the less likely you are to let emotion usurp your judgment and your demeanor. A calm client is not so apt to fume, fuss, or fumble. Remember: The attitude a trial lawyer most appreciates in a client is pretty close to the attitude you like to see in your patients.

Now comes the part of the case when the enemy takes direct aim on your professional competence, as the experts occupy center stage. You will need all your self-control.

Experts come into the scene because, for matters not within the experience and ken of the average juror, the law requires testimony from a person with special training, experience, and skill in the particular area at issue. In any medical-malpractice case, the ultimate question for the jury is, Did the defendant-physician fail to exercise the degree of skill and care of the average physician practicing his specialty at that particular point in time?

Virtually by definition, this is not a question which an unin-

structed layperson could rationally answer. Thus the plaintiff almost certainly will have to call at least one physician, qualified as an expert in your specialty.

This rule is not universal, however, and the definition of "expert" can be quite loose. So long as the testifying witness possesses a medical degree and a license to practice, he may pass muster. The test in some jurisdictions, for example, is simply whether or not the proposed witness has some "special knowledge" which the trier of fact would find useful. In one well-known instance, a state appellate court approved the trial judge's permitting a general practitioner to give an opinion as to the performance of a psychiatrist.

Bear in mind, however, that a judge's merely allowing the physician or any other expert to testify does not constitute a judicial seal of approval on his evidence. A vast difference exists between a lawyer's introducing evidence and a jury's believing it. Testimony (or any other form of evidence) that a judge admits into the case is not necessarily plausible. Admissibility is not tantamount to credibility. When a judge allows counsel to introduce an exhibit, or a particular witness to testify about a particular subject, he is merely following the rules, and not making a statement as to the persuasiveness of the evidence.

It is also a mistake to regard an expert testifying against you as either a renegade or a hired gun. A sardonic doctor once said, "Those who can, practice; those who can't, testify." That is not so, either. You would be much wiser to reach into your store of detachment. Try to regard the other side's expert simply as a professional who happens to disagree with your view of the patient and the best way to handle his medical problems. (As an aid to calm understanding, you might remember that your side, too, will be relying on expert testimony.)

The witness will proffer the opinion in a formulaic context. First, he will respond to questions about his training, background, and experience, with particular reference to the type of procedure or treatment involved in the case at bar. At that point, some judges permit defense counsel to conduct a lim-

ited "cross-examination as to qualifications," restricted to probing the physician's purported expertise. Others defer all cross-examination until the close of direct examination, especially if no one seriously questions the witness's credentials.

After the witness has been "qualified," plaintiff's counsel will endeavor to establish the physician's familiarity with the facts of this particular case. Sometimes, the doctor acquired this knowledge in the course of treating the plaintiff after you did. Frequently, the expert knows about the case only from reviewing the medical documents, including the hospital records (if there are any) and your office notes, which plaintiff's counsel will have obtained, legitimately, in the course of pretrial discovery.

Whatever the source of the expert's knowledge about the patient's treatment, his function in the trial is devastatingly simple. He (alone, or in combination with other witnesses) must persuade the jury that, whatever your overall medical competence, on this particular occasion you acted negligently. He will further try to convince the jurors that your miscues were *a* (not necessarily *the*) proximate cause of the patient's post-treatment problems.

In performing his job, the witness will necessarily have to malign *your* job. One way or another—sometimes more than one way—he will tell the jury that you dropped the medical / surgical ball. How he does it will depend on a mix of factors: the nature of the treatment and whether it lends itself to analysis which a layperson can easily grasp; the witness's testimonial, teaching, and communicating skills; the witness's medical understanding; and, not least important, the degree of your error (or apparent error).

No matter what shape the presentation, at the end of it you will not look good. We tell you this in advance, because the nature of medicine as a profession and the average physician's psychological makeup are such that, once a doctor is past residency, the rarity of harsh public criticism makes *any* imputation of shortcoming extremely threatening and disturbing.

We mentioned this in connection with the litigation's incep-

tion. It will be worse now. When you actually hear a fellow physician opine to a panel of medically ignorant lay people that you have not only erred but caused your patient real harm, you will probably feel so angry and betrayed that sitting motionless requires an immense act of will.

Make the effort. Stay calm. Whether the testimony has moved you to contempt, rage, or scorn, do not let body language, gesture, or facial expression reveal your thoughts. Do not attempt to communicate them to the jury. Do not, however, make the correlative mistake of displaying elaborate nonchalance. The jury, you may be sure, will watch you, to see how you are reacting. Any visible attempt to laugh off the damaging evidence will only lead the jurors to consider you either dim or heartless. Better to convey the quiet certainty of someone who knows that his time will come. In fact, that is exactly so. When the experts have finished, the other side's case is usually complete, and you will hear the lawyer say, "The plaintiff rests."

At this point, the defendant's lawyer ordinarily makes a motion, sometimes in writing, often orally (out of the jury's hearing), seeking to end the case in the physician's favor without further evidence. Usually called a "motion for a directed verdict," it essentially argues that, even if the jury believes all the plaintiff's evidence, the net effect is, as a matter of law, zero.

Defendants espouse such arguments routinely. Just as routinely, judges deny them, because the evidentiary threshold which the plaintiff must cross is so low, and because in almost every case the expert's testimony suffices. Sometimes, the defendant's lawyer will not even bother to argue.

To you, who may regard the expert as an obvious charlatan purveying testimony palpably unbelievable, if not scientifically impossible, your lawyer may appear an incompetent craven. On the contrary, he is probably demonstrating sound professional judgment. Bear in mind that the test now is not whether *you* consider the doctor incredible, nor whether the judge does, nor even whether the jury has been dozing or laughing throughout the expert's stay in the witness box.

Credibility has nothing to do with the judge's decision. The question is only this: Taking all the evidence in the light most favoring *the plaintiff,* drawing only the inferences which help *him,* disregarding all contrary evidence or inferences, *could* (not *would*) a reasonable juror conclude that you had not met the applicable professional standard?

Unless yours is the exceptionally rare case, most defense lawyers would probably feel that pressing a motion to end the case at this point would only delay the proceedings and antagonize the judge. Better to make the gesture and then move on to the much more promising business of laying out for the jury your side of the story.

CHAPTER ELEVEN

Your Turn at Bat: *Primum Non Nocere*

If your attorney did not make an opening statement immediately after the plaintiff's opening, she will do so at the start of the defendant's case. Remember, however, that an opening statement is not supposed to be an argument. Do not, therefore, expect to hear the shade of Clarence Darrow thundering in your defense—at least, not yet. More likely, your attorney will remind the jurors that every story has two sides, and that they have promised to hear the case fully before making a decision. She may also sketch some of what she expects the evidence will show on the question of your professional competence.

Defense of a medical-malpractice action generally encompasses both a major and a minor theme. Usually, most of the effort aims to refute the contention that your performance failed to meet medical norms. If the case concerns failure to inform the patient of the risks the treatment involved, the strategy is to counter the plaintiff's version of what you told her—or failed to tell her.

Secondarily, the defense seeks to implant the suggestion

either that the plaintiff's condition resulted from something besides improper treatment, or that the condition is not so disabling as the plaintiff claims. Success here usually requires a delicate touch. Although a certain amount of exaggeration is endemic to the entire litigation process (on both sides of the "versus"), in most cases, the plaintiff has sustained a demonstrably bad result. Contrary to a strong current of medical folklore, the majority of those who sue for medical malpractice are not fakers. Most have suffered a palpable injury. Whether that injury resulted from anything but misfortune is, of course, another matter.

In setting trial strategy, therefore, astute defense attorneys normally do not use the opening to brand the patient a malingerer, or to do anything much beyond trying to immunize the jury from the plaintiff's opening. Instead, defendant's attorney will concentrate on the *medical* aspects of the defense or (if the case turns on the informed-consent issue) on the conflicting versions of the important pretreatment doctor-patient conversations.

Remember one essential point of law: The burden of proof rests with the plaintiff, and no one else. The defendant does not have to show that she acted with the required skill and care; the defendant does not have to prove she fully informed the plaintiff about the nature and risks of the proposed procedure. Certainly, counsel will introduce evidence, probably including your testimony, to stress the weakness of the plaintiff's case. But she will not undertake to *prove* the correctness of yours. Every experienced trial lawyer knows that almost as great a risk lies in attempting to prove what one need not establish as in failing to prove something essential.

Although of course strategies differ according to the case, the nature of the defense's task—shaking the jury's confidence in the plaintiff's version of the facts and the science—makes plain that the two star witnesses will be you and your expert. Although the order of appearance and the content of the testimony will, again, depend on the strategic situation, the broad outline is fairly predictable. The expert's task is to emphasize the error of the other side's medical argument and,

incidentally, to endorse your performance. Your job is to tell what you did, to show the jury that under the circumstances you made reasonable decisions and choices, and to let the jury know that you are a nice person—or at least not an unpleasant one.

In the course of testifying, you may have occasion to call on your own expertise. If you do, remember that, although part of your job is to avoid losing the case, you are in no way responsible for winning it. Do not try to act as the defense's expert; let the detached specialist do that. In usurping her role, you will almost certainly project an air of self-justification, hardly a posture calculated to win the jury's affection. Beyond that, even though you (and your expert) are persuaded that your professional performance was eminently correct, you may not be very good at explaining just *why* you acted properly. Again, leave that role to the person brought in to play it.

Finally, although we hesitate to suggest it, perhaps you are not so expert as you think you are, or, rather, as a top-notch *witness* must be. Nothing destroys a malpractice defense more thoroughly than a defendant who demonstrates her own ignorance. Nothing is more painful for the defense than an arrogant physician self-destructing under the weight of her own ego during a skillful cross-examination.

All that being said, however, we do not mean to suggest that you should abandon your medical training when you take the stand. If at appropriate times a correct answer requires rendering an expert opinion, you may, and probably should, do so. Your lawyer will let you know beforehand when such a situation is likely to arise. We merely caution that you await the occasion, rather than seeking it out, and that you limit your display to what is necessary.

In any event, when donning the expert's mantle, remember that, although in that capacity your job is to teach, as *defendant* your aim is to win the jury's esteem. Thus your mode should be friendly, unpedantic, and low-key. Above all, you do not wish to lose any ground. If you can make some points with the jury, fine. Never forget, however, that a triumphant dem-

onstration of your expertise is not worth antagonizing even a single juror.

Be aware at all times not merely of what you are saying, but of how you are saying it. The object is to win over the jurors to you _as a person,_ not necessarily as a brilliant medico. When you explain a technical point, always remember the nature of your listeners. They are not physicians or even medical students. What passes in the medical-school classroom or hospital lounge for unsurpassed clarity may leave a lay jury hopelessly befuddled. A technically flawless and precise exposition that would draw applause from a professional review board may strike jurors as jargon-heavy boasting.

For a physician testifying in her own defense, a textbook vocabulary can be the kiss of death. Why not adopt instead the KISS of wisdom? KISS, as in Keep It Short and Simple. At the same time, avoid even the suggestion of condescension. Thus, do not say, "The patient presented a manifest comminuted epicondylar fracture." Much better to say, "Ms. Smith's elbow was obviously shattered." Do it naturally, avoiding any intimation that what you have to say is so arcane that none but the initiated could possibly understand the concept without special interpretation.

That last example raised an incidental point worth emphasizing. Physicians, particularly males, have a habit of falling into first-name familiarity with patients almost immediately upon initial contact. This tendency extends beyond direct address. Thus doctors testifying will frequently say things like, "Freddy was making excellent progress." We have even seen hospital-record entries to the same effect: "Bonita was instructed to return for re-examination in two weeks."

Whatever may be your custom elsewhere, this kind of casualness can cause grave problems in court, making the witness appear insensitive and condescending. More and more, judges are endeavoring to eliminate this particular practice, because many people—and, by definition, many jurors—find it offensive, especially if the patient happens to be a female or a minority of either gender. The better course is to refer to everyone older than fourteen as "Mr." if male and as "Ms." if

female. Prudence also suggests exercising caution in the use of "boy" or "girl."

When your lawyer has finished direct examination, plaintiff's attorney will have a chance to cross-examine (actually, a renewed chance, if she brought you to the stand as part of plaintiff's own case). Most judges will limit the cross-examination to matters not covered in your earlier grilling or to new matters brought out for the first time during your own attorney's direct examination. In either event, from your standpoint, the testimonial principles are the same. Everything we said on this score in Chapter Nine also applies now.

Remember, you are a witness, not a lawyer or a judge. If you think a question is unfair or even legally improper, resist the urge to tell the interrogator so. Pause before you answer, to give your attorney a chance to object. If your attorney does not speak up, consider that she may have a valid tactical reason for remaining silent. Lawyers are, for example, acutely aware that jurors resent a constant stream of "Objection!" and that the resentment frequently rubs off onto the objectionable attorney and (worse) her client.

Many times, therefore, even though a question violates some rule of evidence, counsel will ignore the defect. That, of course, leaves you in the position of having to respond to an inquiry which even a nonlawyer like you recognizes as improper. Answer it anyhow, if a fair answer is possible; if not, calmly tell your interrogator that you cannot answer the question "the way you have put it." Do not, however, add gratuitously, "and would you like me to tell you why?" If counsel wants to bring out the reason for your inability, she will ask. Respond plainly, simply, and briefly.

Never appeal directly to the judge for a ruling; that is the lawyer's job. Many judges resent a witness's sidestepping counsel. Many jurors regard a witness who does something like that as arrogant and out of line. Taking tough questions is part of the general unpleasantness that testifying imposes on most witnesses, physicians or not.

Even if her conduct is flatly outrageous, never, at any time, allow yourself to enter a shouting match with the plaintiff's

attorney. With the jury avidly taking in the whole undignified wrangle, even if you win, you lose.

Another likely hazard is the written—more precisely, the printed—word. The reason is simple. Except for the most basic medical principles, every rule of treatment has its exceptions; and a careful medical author will say so. Thus, no matter how comprehensive the treatise, no matter how erudite the author, *any* written discussion of *any* medical topic is bound to contain language which, without distortion, can be understood to criticize, modify, or qualify any particular medical procedure or treatment.

If the cross-examiner knows enough not to push her luck, a textbook (whoever the author) can become a potent forensic weapon. The technique seems ingenuous; in the hands of a skillful advocate, it proceeds with a courtesy all the more devastating because the gentle manner masks the menace.

Here are a couple of examples.

Suppose the plaintiff presented to the defendant-physician by telephone, reporting fever in the 100°–101° range, with slight dry cough, headaches, and stiffness in the neck area. "Sounds like 'flu," says the doctor, thinking of the dozen similar cases she has actually seen in her office during the past week, as well as the twenty patients who have reported identical symptoms over the phone. "Stay in bed, drink lots of fluids, and take two aspirin every four hours to help the discomfort and the fever. If things don't improve in a couple of days, let me hear from you."

Within twenty-four hours, the patient is in the emergency room, with a plain diagnosis of meningitis, followed by serious complications, followed by a lawsuit. At trial, the defendant-physician faces a series of questions something like this:

> **Q.** At the time you were making the long-distance diagnosis, you had available to you a book by Dr. Dolores Tick called *Practical Medicine,* did you not?
> **A.** Yes.
> **Q.** And we can fairly say, can we not, that Dr. Tick is a well-

known authority on the general practice of medicine as it applies to communicable diseases?

A. She is well respected, yes.

Q. And you yourself often refer to her book, isn't that so?

A. Whenever I think I need to.

Q. Can we take it that you refer to Dr. Tick's book because it gives accurate scientific information and advice on which you, as a practicing physician, can and do rely?

A. Yes.

Q. Are you aware that on page 102 of *Practical Medicine* Dr. Tick says: "The familiar constellation of symptoms comprising above-100° fever, dry cough, and muscular aches commonly referred to as 'the flu' can easily mask more serious illness"?

A. I don't have the book in front of me, but I'll take your word for it.

Q. Well, with Her Honor's permission, I'll come to the witness box with my copy and we can read together.

THE COURT: Go ahead.

Q. And doesn't Dr. Tick go on to say: ". . . particularly at a time of so-called epidemic, when the sheer number of patients presenting identical symptoms may provoke the assumption that they are all similarly afflicted, caution and discriminating inquiry must be the prudent physician's watchwords"? Did I read that correctly?

A. Yes.

Q. But when my client called and told you about the fever, the stiff neck, and the cough, you didn't ask any more questions, did you?

A. I didn't think they were necessary.

Q. And that's because you assumed that what was producing the symptoms was the same thing, the same 'flu, that dozens of your other patients had. Right?

A. I formed a medical judgment that she had the so-called 'flu.

Observe how skillful questioning has (a) turned the text-book's counsel of caution into a rule of practice; and (b) driven

the doctor to admit violating the "rule." No, the doctor never actually conceded ignoring the precept. Actually, from a forensic point of view, she did worse, because she tried to weasel out of an admission which, in light of the textbook's language, most jurors would probably have expected her to make. Thus she runs the risk of projecting as not only careless but shifty.

What to do? Not much, except to answer "Yes" or "No" whenever possible. Even the last answer, which seems to put the doctor in a better light, in fact causes difficulty. A good lawyer will not press the matter further at that time. In clos-ing argument, however, when the doctor cannot offer any rebuttal, the lawyer is likely to say: "You heard the defen-dant's own words. She formed a 'medical judgment' that the patient had 'flu. Some judgment, ladies and gentlemen. No tests, no examination, no nothing. Not even a thought that, as the great book by Dr. Tick says, the book the defendant relies on, plainly warns, those symptoms can hide serious ill-ness." And so on.

A second example makes the point in a slightly different way. Observe, as you read it, how the doctor's answers fre-quently prolong the agony.

 Q. Doctor, as a board-certified urologist, are you familiar with a textbook by Dr. Hugo Dailey called *Urology*?
 A. Yes.
 Q. And would you agree with me that it's used in many medical schools, to teach medical students about urol-ogy?
 A. Well, I don't know how many, but it's certainly well-rec-ognized. [*Note:* An excellent example, by the way, of how not to answer; the response was complete after the word "many."]
 Q. And we can agree, can we not, that Dr. Dailey's text-book, used in many medical schools, is authoritative on the subject of urology?
 A. Yes. [*Note:* "Authoritative" here means that those in the profession consider it an authority, and consequently rely

on its accuracy. Unless you regard the entire book in that light, do not accept the characterization. However, if you think that only part of the book is authoritative, shape your answer accordingly. On the other hand, if the whole book truly is authoritative, your least damaging answer is a simple unqualified "Yes."]

Q. Now, doctor, you have testified that prostate cancer is not a problem for men under the age of twenty-five, isn't that so? [*Note:* This is one of those double questions: (1) Did you so testify? (2) Whether you did or not, is the substantive statement correct?]

A. Yes, I said that.

Q. Now, just let me show you *Urology,* Dr. Dailey's authoritative textbook, and ask you to turn to page 85, which I've marked with a slip of paper.

A. Yes.

Q. About halfway down the page, does Dr. Dailey write: "Males under twenty-five rarely present with full-scale prostatic cancer"? Have I read that correctly?

A. Yes.

Q. And does the next sentence say, "But when it does appear, the prognosis is almost always grave"?

A. Yes.

Q. And if you could help us with the translation, Doctor, what Dr. Dailey is saying in his textbook is: When a young man under twenty-five gets cancer of the prostate, his chances aren't good; isn't that what Dr. Dailey is saying?

A. Well, I'm not sure I can agree with that. [A simple "Yes" is the best course.]

Q. Doctor, doesn't "grave prognosis" mean: The condition is serious and the young man's chances aren't very good?

A. I don't mean to fence with you [*Note:* Nonetheless, that is exactly what the doctor is doing], but Dr. Dailey's words are "the prognosis is almost always grave."

Q. Sure. And "prognosis" means "forecast," or "prediction," or "probable outcome," right?

A. Yes.

Q. And "grave" means "serious" or "grim"?

A. I don't know about "grim."

Q. "Bad news"?

A. Certainly not good news. [*Note:* Better, three answers back, to have said "Yes."]

Q. And it's not good news because a young man with a cancerous prostate faces either death from the disease, or treatment which even if it's successful may well leave the patient with a lifetime of urinary problems and impotence, isn't that right?

A. Well, you're putting it rather strongly. [*Note:* Far better just to answer "Yes."]

Q. Have I said anything incorrect?

A. I guess not.

Q. So, Doctor, to get back to what you testified on direct, do you still want this jury to believe that a twenty-five-year-old man facing a serious forecast of bad news because he has prostatic cancer, with the prospect of permanent impotence and a lifetime of difficulty urinating, has no problems? [*Note:* Just say "No." *Primum non nocere.*]

The moral of these unpleasant little scenarios is simple: If the book is well recognized as authoritative, and if it appears to condemn your professional behavior on the occasion in question, concede the point as gracefully and as expeditiously as possible. Sometimes a doctor will try to ease the sting by admitting only that the book is "helpful," not "authoritative." The witness would apparently rather be seen as spurning help than as flouting authority. We leave the choice to you. Whatever your locution, remember, a treatise does not compel the jury to reach any particular result; moreover, what the jury thinks of you (or the plaintiff) may frequently matter more than whether on this particular occasion you practiced medicine literally by the book.

During one trial we recall, the issue was a surgeon's carelessness, and the prime evidence an X-ray plate of the patient's lower abdomen taken three days postop. It disclosed, with the stark contrast that metal always displays in a radiological setting, a thirteen-inch ribbon retractor.

Because the patient had died (from a cause totally unre-
lated to the procedure), the plaintiff was his widow, the exe-
cutrix of his estate. The physician's testimony had been at
best inconclusive; after all, retractors do not normally appear
in a well-sutured incision. Still, nothing he said had added to
the damage. The widow, on the other hand, had presented as
a woman locked in a bad marriage who looked forward, at
last, to getting something from her deceased and (in her view)
worthless husband. The contrast in personalities struck every-
one—especially, perhaps, the jurors, who returned a defen-
dant's verdict. On the defendant's attorney's office wall now
hangs a framed thirteen-inch ribbon retractor.

Remember: Your personality sometimes matters more than
your performance.

Does Misery Really Love Company?

Suppose yours is not the only name to the right of the "versus." Although frequently a patient will sue only the treating physician, in many cases, particularly those involving surgery or some other hospital procedure, the plaintiff aims at a group of targets. Thus, if the patient alleges that the defendant failed to meet the standards of a reasonably competent anesthesiologist, the list of defendants will also include the hospital, the anesthesiology resident, any nurse likely to have played a significant role in anesthetizing the patient, and (depending on the facts) possibly the surgeon.

People may regard this net-spreading as anything from sadism to overkill to thoroughness, depending on the point of view. Hard though it may be for any member of the defendant group to accept, a careful attorney always tries to make sure that he has brought into the case every person or organization who / which might in any way share responsibility for the plaintiff's injury. No lawyer, and certainly no client, wants to learn after an unfavorable verdict that the jury felt that the plaintiff ought to win, "but we just didn't see how any of the

defendants was responsible; how come you didn't sue X?"

Of course X is always someone the plaintiff's attorney thought the evidence completely exonerated. Defense counsel probably shared that assessment; nonetheless, he took every opportunity to suggest in one way or another that X, although missing, was the true culprit.

The realities of litigation in this situation are such that invariably, when the verdict comes in, the statutorily allowed time to sue X has long since passed. Worse, because hospital personnel and young doctors share the general population's mobility, the odds are excellent that at this point X has moved out of state—or, in these days of extranational residencies, even out of the country. True, one can track X down and commence suit, but the cost is great, the difficulty of assembling the cast in a distant location substantial, and the other side's home-court advantage incalculable. Rather than run these risks, therefore, the lawyer will try to line up all the ducks the first time around; you may well find yourself with company in the bull's-eye.

Being a codefendant requires you to give your position some thought and attention. To begin with, in most cases, you will notice that each defendant has a separate lawyer. Although you may regard this as merely an attempt to multiply fees, the reasons are a good deal more significant. However close they may be in their personal and professional relations— indeed, even if the same insurer covers all of them—the defendants' individual interests now are mutually antagonistic. True, they all would be quite content to see the plaintiff recover nothing against anybody. But if that is not to happen, then everyone hopes: "Whoever loses, let it not be me."

Although this is, of course, a perfectly natural desire, it does make every defendant in the moment of truth the enemy (or at least not the friend) of everybody else. Almost certainly, that will require you to recast your normal instincts. We do not suggest you emulate Ishmael (from the Old Testament, not from *Moby Dick*) and turn your hand against every man— or woman. Nor need you fear that everyone's hand threatens

you. Still, as we have had occasion to remark before, a little paranoia can have its uses.

The first rule is easy to state and hard to follow: Never discuss the case with anyone except your spouse or significant other unless your lawyer is present. That old devil casual conversation can lay you out flat. Relaxing over a drink, trying to make sense of the mess that has suddenly been thrown on you, you confide to your old pal, a longtime co-worker, now a codefendant, that, yes, you might very well have missed that diagnosis.

Do not faint with astonishment and rage when, while on the stand, he tells the jury in sparse, stark detail every word you let slip over the soothing beverage. Any testimony about what you told him is not inadmissible hearsay: it is *your* statement that he is relating. Even if it qualifies as hearsay, it still comes into evidence, because you were saying something contrary to your own interest—namely, conceding that you had miscued.

Casual conversation is Out. The second rule follows a similar path: Negotiating is also Out, because bargaining is strictly lawyers' work. How about professional talk? Well, if you and a codefendant work together, you certainly should not stop communicating—about the work. Be alert, however, lest shop talk slide into case talk. Separate the lawsuit from your everyday life and conversations. It can be done, even between close professional colleagues. Joe Tinker and Johnny Evers turned all those double plays ("Tinker to Evers to Chance") and never said a word to each other off the field.

What happens if you come up with an idea that you believe will help a codefendant, while not causing you any difficulty (or so you think)? The answer is easy: Tell your lawyer, and let him make the tactical decision.

Suppose you learn some helpful information; can you share it? Yes, but only with your lawyer.

How about getting a little help from a friend or mentor, someone lacking all connection with the case? Surely, it must be all right to put the facts to him, just for his insights. Sorry.

As you have probably guessed, our response is still the same: Let your lawyer obtain the helpful expert opinion. If you want to suggest the name of a physician who might be worth talking to, feel free to let your lawyer know. If he thinks the contact will be of assistance, *he* will follow up. For your part, accept the professional's judgment. If he decides not to talk to your "discovery," do not take the decision as a personal rejection.

All this may sound like an endless tape, but the point is crucial, and bears repeating. Let your lawyer do your fighting *and* your negotiating, even with your fellow defendants. Although attorneys do not regard it as a term of approbation, the pejorative "mouthpiece" rests on a foundation of common sense: Until the lawsuit is done, over, finished, and history, the lawyer, and no one but the lawyer, does all your talking about the case—to friends, as well as to enemies.

Mid-Trial Settlement: Frustration or Fulfillment?

Something near 96 percent of all civil cases—including, of course, lawsuits having nothing to do with medical malpractice—reach a mutually acceptable result at some point before final judgment. The operative phrase is "mutually acceptable," not "happy," or "desirable," or "advantageous," or even "satisfactory." Moreover, "before final judgment" covers the entire life of the case, from before the patient's lawyer even files suit papers, up until the jury delivers its verdict. Indeed, it is not unheard of, although rare, for the parties to reach agreement after the appellate process has started.

Chapter Six covered the general concept of settlement *before* trial; now you must deal with the idea of in-court compromise, or what you may consider battlefield surrender. Although the principles are the same in both situations, the timing can raise sensitive emotional issues.

Bear in mind that a great many health-care cases never present the settlement issue. If, after thoroughly analyzing the claim and the physician's conduct, the insurance group has taken the firm position that it will *never* voluntarily pay the

plaintiff anything, or even make an offer, the settlement issue will not enter the courtroom, or the courthouse corridors.

Right now, though, our subject is not the "no-pay" case but, rather, the lawsuit in which, although settlement talks have broken down or never begun, the parties are willing to consider the subject *at the right moment.*

Identifying the right moment is a matter of some delicacy, because in litigation, as in many professional situations, experts can differ. If, however, we temporarily put aside questions of bargaining strategy, and similarly disregard every lawyer's reluctance to appear "chicken" by being first to mention the "s" word, the most common reason for deferring settlement consideration until mid-trial is the desire, in the lawyers' phrase, to see how the parties "look on the stand."

In context, this does not refer to physical appearance, although, as we have earlier commented, the way a person presents as a witness can significantly affect the outcome. Rather, the "look" connotes the witness's apparent total effect on jury, judge, and anticipated verdict. A good lawyer will also ponder the potential influence which the testimonial performances may have on the opponent's evaluation. Whatever mix of factors counsel takes into consideration, you can be sure that the respective impacts of the defendant (i.e., you) and the plaintiff will form a significant element.

The dynamics of this process are, from the attorneys' viewpoint, defined by two questions: Does the jury appear to be accepting the plaintiff's testimony or rejecting it? Does the jury seem to be accepting the defendant's testimony or rejecting it? (The lawyers, of course, also try to answer the subsidiary query: How persuasive do the jurors seem to have found any other witness, particularly, but not exclusively, whatever experts may have given evidence?)

Here as elsewhere, simplicity of definition may mask complexity of application. Estimating the mid-trial value of a case calls for subtle judgment, based on experience. No one, no matter how case-hardened in "the pit" of litigation, is an expert. Unlike a horse-race handicapper, a lawyer cannot inform her judgment by consulting the jury's or the parties' previous

record. Unlike an investment adviser, the attorney cannot rely on hard, quantifiable data, or indeed on any data at all. In short, although the enterprise necessarily entails serious consequences, a lawyer evaluates a case's prospects by nothing more than impressionistic, subjective guesstimation.

Whatever its genesis, all the calculation, possibility-weighing, and unabashed mumbo-jumbo will produce an evaluation which, if unfavorable, is likely to irritate an exquisitely sensitive part of any litigant's psyche, plaintiff or defendant. No matter how tactfully the lawyer presents the assessment, the client experiences a disquieting amalgam of betrayal and anger. Your own lawyer, the champion of your honor and your professional future, will seem to have deserted you. She, of course, will regard it as merely furnishing an honest, professional appraisal, a candid picture of reality, of "the way things are going."

You are both justified. But the justification is irrelevant to solving the problem at hand. Feelings, honest though they be, must yield to the iron necessity of the situation. No place or time for soft soap here. A hard-headed—indeed, hard-nosed—sometimes brutally frank evaluation is the medication of choice. If your lawyer believes the jury is falling in love with the plaintiff, she will tell you. Even though you are certain that the sniveling little wretch of a plaintiff fell flat on her testimonial prat, if the lawyer reads the jurors otherwise, neither your emotional disagreement nor your hurt feelings will prevent her saying so.

Worse, from your ego's standpoint, if she thinks the jurors are giving your witness-box performance two thumbs down, she will express that opinion, to you and to the insurance representative (either by telephone or, if the latter has been attending the trial, in person). Not all your piety, nor all your wit, nor even your distress can lure her back to cancel any part of the bad review.

In short, one way or another, the lawyer is taking a detached, professional view of the case. Given your lack of litigation experience and the heavy emotional investment any malpractice defendant (like any other litigant) necessarily must make,

no one expects you to match the attorney's evaluative ability. It might not be a bad idea, however, to understand the frame of reference and, perhaps, to try adopting it, even temporarily. To paraphrase what the French philosopher Pascal wrote in a slightly different connection: Say the words often enough, and pretty soon you may be speaking the language.

When a lawyer (or an insurance professional) evaluates a case, she is always considering one fundamental question: How can I get the client (or the company) out of this for the lowest possible expenditure? Total victory—i.e., a verdict of no malpractice—is certainly a consummation devoutly to be wished. It is not, however, the dominant goal. Rather, the lawyer and the insurer are much more concerned about the reverse of a defendant's verdict: a large recovery by the plaintiff, or what the personal-injury bar calls "the big hit." Insurance adjusters do not fall asleep to dreams of sugarplum no-liability verdicts. They do most assuredly wake up at 3:00 a.m. sweating over the whopping, headline-creating, megaverdict. Not even the encouraging trial-result statistics (80 percent for defendants) can sedate them.

All this concern to avoid a major loss focuses on something called "exposure." Exposure is the highest dollar figure that the evaluator estimates the plaintiff can obtain in the absence of intolerable jury prejudice. ("Intolerable" is not a mere pejorative. The test whether a verdict is too high as a matter of law, not just as a matter of opinion, is whether, taking all the evidence into consideration, and viewing all questions in the light which most favors the *plaintiff*, the judge nonetheless finds that the number shocks her conscience. Although this appears to give the judge an unbounded discretion, in practice, before a judge will alter a jury verdict, she must be reasonably sure that it will also offend the appellate court.)

A lawyer sizing up settlement potential therefore begins by assuming that the jury will "find liability"; that is, that the jurors will regard the physician's conduct as having failed to meet average standards of performance—in short, that she was negligent, and that the negligence caused the patient's

injury. Thus the lawyer takes malpractice as a given, and proceeds directly to the numbers.

Evaluation of exposure requires the lawyer to put herself into the jurors' minds and so to deduce what they could conceivably conclude the plaintiff is entitled to receive. Some of the calculus is objective, even arithmetical. The medical and hospital bills, for instance, are usually not subject to much dispute.

A deliberate pessimism guides consideration of the other "special damages" (the legal term for items like lost wages, extra expense of home help—in short, anything directly expressible in dollars or as an out-of-pocket payment, whether the pocket be the plaintiff's or the health insurer's). Whether any particular expense is attributable to the injury caused by the assumed negligence is much less definite. For purposes of estimating *exposure,* however, the lawyer will again take the darkest view. In a death case, where the patient's spouse or family are claiming that the malpractice caused her death, the funeral and burial expenses make up an additional element of special damages.

Even though an insurance company or a health-care plan may have paid for an item of expense, the plaintiff is still entitled to recover an equivalent amount from the defendant. Although you probably regard this as unconscionable, the rule rests on a simple, sound rationale. Any windfall should benefit the injured person, rather than the person who caused the injury. Frequently, the insurer or plan can in turn obtain reimbursement from the patient, which tends to limit the windfall. That, however, is another question, which legally and practically neither concerns nor affects you. In California, as a matter of fact, a statute explicitly permits telling the jurors about the "collateral" insurance, for their consideration when assessing damages.

In dealing with any variety of damages, you should keep in mind a few easily understood commonsense principles. (Incidentally, the word can be construed as either plural or singular. "Damage" denotes the harm itself, "damages" the effect of the harm expressed in dollar terms.)

The first rule is that the defendant "takes the plaintiff as he finds her." Suppose a physician negligently and wrongly prescribes a particular drug which *in the dosage administered* would not adversely affect a normal person. *This* patient, however, unknown to the doctor, is idiosyncratically sensitive to the medicine, and accordingly sustains injury. Legally, the physician cannot avoid liability.

Second, a defendant is not responsible for damages traceable to the patient's pre-existing condition, rather than to the sequelae of the negligent treatment. Suppose an automobile accident rendered the patient paraplegic years before she presented to the defendant-surgeon for treatment of a cervical bone spur totally unrelated to the old injury. In the course of surgery, the doctor's negligence injured the spinal cord, and the patient left the operating room a quadriplegic. Legally, the surgeon is responsible only for the damages representing the difference between paraplegia and quadriplegia, not for the difference between full health and quadriplegia.

Third, if the negligence aggravated or exacerbated a prior condition, the defendant does have to answer for the consequences of the exacerbation. Consider a patient with acne. If a dermatologist negligently prescribes an ointment which not only fails to alleviate the acne but makes it worse, the physician is liable for those damages attributable to the worsening.

In summary, a defendant must pay for any and all effects of her own carelessness, but not for any effects which that negligence did not cause.

Your attorney, with due reference to the principles we have just mentioned, factors in the special damages and turns to an evaluation of the subjective damages: pain and suffering; scarring (if any); loss of function (if any); diminished enjoyment of life; loss of support and society (if the case involves a consortium claim); loss of psychological, fiscal, and moral support (if the malpractice caused the patient's death). If in your state a plaintiff can recover *punitive* damages—designed, as the name implies, to punish the defendant—the attorney will also consider them.

Given the inherently unquantifiable nature of all these ele-

ments, how can an attorney—or anyone else not gifted with clairvoyance—possibly determine the amount that a jury will decide? If "determine" means "calculate," the honest answer is: She cannot; nor can anyone else.

Gauging the settlement value of a case, however, does not require micrometrics. It depends instead on experience, judgment, and an instinctive ability to guess how *this* jury will probably evaluate *this* patient / doctor / evidence. In short, the process is neither a science nor a knack; Judge Learned Hand once called it "a black art," which is probably as apt a description as the nature of the exercise permits.

Having established what she regards as a realistic dollar exposure, the lawyer then discounts the number by her estimate of the plaintiff's recovery chances. We must emphasize again that this requires a cold-blooded, or at least cool-headed, evaluation of the evidence, including—perhaps especially— the apparent effectiveness of each witness who has testified up to that point in the trial. In that respect, the lawyer is a catcher during a mid-game mound conference, telling the manager, while the pitcher listens, that the last three pitches came to the plate like grapefruit, and that the pitcher is hopelessly out of gas.

A somewhat more acute analogy might be this: The lawyer telling the client that the case is not going well is like a physician telling a patient that because conservative treatment has failed, surgery is necessary. Each speaker merely gives an honest professional judgment; and each recipient tends to blame the bad tidings on the messenger.

Malpractice litigation does raise another issue, far removed from the merits of the case. As you know, since September 1, 1990, every payment to a malpractice claimant, no matter when it occurs, no matter what the reason, must be reported to the National Practitioner Data Bank. That in itself may provide *you* a valid reason for not settling. If your insurance policy gives you veto power, your views will prevail. Even if the company retains final say, normally the settlement will not go forward without giving you a chance to express your views.

In either event, you would be well advised to make your

response reflective, rather than reflexive. The question is not whether the reporting requirement will work to your professional disadvantage; we can take as given that you would be better off without it. Unfortunately, once any patient makes a claim, reporting becomes mandatory unless the claim drops (unlikely) or the jury finds in the physician's favor.

That last alternative, however, is exactly what the mid-trial evaluation has in essence rejected. By the time defense counsel has decided to recommend settlement, she has, after detailed analysis, concluded either that the chance of a defendant's verdict is nil, or that the risk of heavy loss so outweighs the slim chance of victory as to leave no viable option but settlement. The possibilities no longer include exoneration; the sole remaining issue is monetary. The best medical analogy is gangrene. Once the diagnosis is established, the only open questions are when and how to undertake surgery. The certainty that the operation will entail mutilation plays no further part in the decisional process.

To sum up the whole difficult subject: An attorney's mid-case settlement recommendation simply amounts to a suggestion that the client cut the apparently inevitable losses. It is in no sense a condemnation of the physician's moral or professional conduct. Just as a wise patient accepts unpleasant news and seeks to work *with* the doctor in ameliorating the situation, so a wise albeit disappointed physician-client will try to accept the grim litigational picture with understanding and calm.

CHAPTER FOURTEEN

The Beginning of the End

For the participants, especially the parties, the hardest part of the trial comes after the evidence has closed—that is, after both sides have "rested." No more witnesses; no more exhibits. The case, however, is far from over. Wrung out though the parties may be from the events so far, the litigants still have to face worse.

The changing fortunes of a trial, where hope plays team-tag with despair, and angry doubt blends with serene certitude, nonetheless afford the parties some feeling of being able to affect the outcome, marginal though their influence may be. After all, merely passing a note to one's attorney creates the illusion of actually helping him point the artillery.

In the end-game stages of a trial, however, all pretense of participation ends. From the moment the courtroom rings with the words "All parties rest," plaintiff and defendant become nothing but spectators, lacking even the comfort which indifference often brings. The end of the trial now shapes itself through a series of well-defined ceremonies.

At the close of the plaintiff's case, the defendant's lawyer

argued a motion for a directed verdict. He claimed that, even taking all the evidence in a light completely favoring the plaintiff, no reasonable juror could vote for liability. The judge denied the motion, and the case went on.

Now, after the defendant's evidence has also come in, the lawyer renews the motion. He does not do this out of a belief that the defendant's presentation has so weakened the plaintiff's case that plaintiff is legally bound to lose. The most-favorable-light standard still applies. However, the rules of procedure which most courts follow (adapted from the federal practice) require the directed-verdict motion as a predicate for later review of the trial.

Even when the plaintiff's case seems technically shaky, most judges will reserve decision. If the subsequent jury verdict reflects this negative assessment, nothing more needs to be done. If, however, the jury finds for the plaintiff, the judge can consider the whole matter under calmer circumstances, aided by the parties' thorough memoranda and his own research and reflection. If he then decides that he should have "directed the plaintiff out," he can allow the motion retroactively, and enter judgment for the defendant. Should the appellate court disagree, it will merely order the original verdict reinstated. The parties will not have to go through another trial.

The next ritual deals with the content of the judge's charge or instruction to the jurors on the legal rules which must govern their deliberations. In every state, the judge is obliged to instruct the jury. Counsel need say nothing. They are, however, entitled to input, if they wish to give it. The rules permit the lawyers to ask that the judge give particular instructions, or that he state the governing principles in one or another choice of words. The judge is not bound to adopt counsel's precise language. If, however, the request states the principle correctly, the judge has to communicate the substance of it to the jury. In any event, the federal procedure and that of most states entitle counsel to learn, *before* they begin arguments, whether the judge will charge as requested.

The lawyer-judge colloquy sometimes takes place out of the

courtroom (although on the record) or at the bench. If, as often happens, the lawyers address the judge in open court, where everyone can hear, the whole business will probably strike you as dull and incomprehensible, and will re-emphasize that major decisions affecting your life neither require nor permit your participation. On the other hand, if the case raises a novel legal point, your attorney will probably have at least sketched its content and significance to you earlier; you may find the process not wholly without interest. At any rate, it does not usually take long.

Now comes the part of the trial that most closely resembles what you see in the movies or on television: closing arguments. Although in some states the plaintiff argues first, most of the time the defendant's counsel, your lawyer, is first up. His job is not to convince the jury that your handling of the case compared favorably with the best of Osler, Cushing, or Paul Dudley White. Remember, the defendant's side almost never has any obligation to prove anything. Instead, the plaintiff bears the burden of persuading the jury that you were negligent. Focus on this point; a good lawyer never forgets it. Your attorney, therefore, will not try to paint you as anyone would like to be painted. Rather, he will suggest that the other side has not succeeded in depicting your professional conduct as legally insufficient.

So far, in what we might call the head-to-head battle, the courtroom atmosphere has been rather low-key, largely because defending counsel relies on logic and moderation, or at least tries to eliminate emotion from the jury's deliberations. When the plaintiff's lawyer takes the lectern, the tempo of the drama increases measurably; you will probably have to refasten your mental seat belt. Be warned: If the lawyer is doing his job, he will sketch a portrait that does not flatter you. You may even think it a distortion, a caricature, or at the very least an unrecognizable and incomplete stick-figure.

Argument styles vary. Some trial lawyers prefer the gentle touch: "The defendant is usually a very careful physician, thoughtful, caring, and compassionate. Unfortunately, even very careful people are sometimes careless. That's what hap-

pened to the defendant; and that's why my client ended up getting sicker instead of better. Maybe the defendant was careless just this once. Maybe he never will be again. Let's hope so. But meanwhile, as a result of *this* unfortunate lapse, my client is left with a condition that will never get better. As between the careless doctor and the totally innocent, trusting patient, who should have to accept responsibility?" And so forth. In the hands and voice of an experienced lawyer who knows what he is doing, the quiet approach can leave the jurors nodding in sympathetic agreement. (Done improperly, it can of course set them nodding with soporific unanimity.) At the other end of the forensic spectrum, we find the kind of attorney who disbelieves in the average juror's susceptibility to a subtle approach. This sort goes straight for the jugular—yours—and, verbally, at least, never lets go. Some sophisticated tastes find the bombast unpersuasive. When embedded in a framework of logic and apt references to the evidence, it can turn a jury into the children of Hamelin.

One thing is certain. Scalpel or machete, caress or bruise, the closing argument has only one purpose: making the jurors think of you as a medical bumbler, and stimulating them to award high damages. On that last point, in many states, the jury never learns the amount that the plaintiff is claiming; its decision on damages must come exclusively from evaluating the evidence. Elsewhere, the rules are looser, and counsel can urge specific figures, even writing them on the blackboard during argument.

Whatever the lawyer's technique arguing damages or liability, you will probably not find it admirable. No one likes to have his flaws publicly dissected and priced, particularly if the dissection comes distressingly close to the mark. The critique becomes even more intolerable when the subject of the analysis must remain not merely mute but visibly unaffected.

No matter what the lawyer says or does, you cannot allow yourself to react, even facially. Perhaps you will hear your medical ability, your character, your concern for the patient twisted and maligned, at least in your view. Perhaps the lawyer will spin a web of what you consider half-truths and unfair

inferences. It does not matter. You must neither stir, smirk, nor scowl.

Perhaps the lawyer will point a damning finger at you while calling on the jury to remember that "this—this *doctor,* who was supposed to cure my client, instead, by disregarding elementary, basic, well-known medical concepts, turned him into the pathetic creature you saw in court." Your anger will surge and you will want to stand and shout, "That's a filthy lie, and you know it!" Let the moment pass. Keep your mouth shut and your features composed. Resist even the impulse to "communicate" with the jurors by a sad how-can-he-say-such-things smile or a gallant you-know-that's-not-true shrug.

In short, sit and take it. Unfortunately, you cannot escape the ordeal by staying out of the courtroom. The jury would certainly notice your absence (especially after you had attended every other minute of the trial) and would probably mark you down for not being able to endure criticism. Be assured, however, that the agony will end, to be replaced by a kind of despairing boredom as the judge begins to give the jurors their final instructions on the principles which will guide their deliberations: the legal standards (for example, what does "negligence" mean?); the factual issues (was the doctor negligent?); the side which must persuade them on each particular issue; and the degree of proof required.

Cynics have referred to this part of the case as "the final argument." It is true that jurors do pay great attention to the charge, and they frequently try to "psych out" the judge in an effort to determine how he *wants* them to decide the case. Judges, however, take particular pains to avoid dictating the result, even in the federal courts, where—unlike the practice in most states—the judge may express an opinion about the evidence, so long as he tells the jurors plainly that they may disregard what he says on that score.

As you saw in Chapter Seven, the charge is, from the appellate court's viewpoint, the most important part of the case. Only rarely is a verdict reversed on appeal simply because the judge mistakenly admitted or excluded evidence. When, however, the higher court perceives what it takes to be a misstate-

ment of the law by the trial judge, reversal is much more likely. Remember, in our system of law, alterations in the basic rules come only gradually. Appellate courts act only after a trial judge has acted; they do not offer suggestions in advance or advisory opinions on coming legal trends. The most apt vehicle for effecting an incremental change in an existing legal principle is review of a jury charge.

Because trial judges understand the importance with which their superiors regard jury instructions, many actually use a prepared text. In some states, the judge *must* adopt "pattern" instructions, which the local supreme court has drafted and preapproved. Elsewhere, the judge is free to select his own language, so long as it accurately expounds the existing rules.

Not all judges, even in states that permit a certain literary freedom, are content to rely on their unaided creativity and memory. Many therefore commit their remarks to writing, and recite the finished product to the jury. Some even send the written instructions to the jury room, so the jurors can consult them during deliberation. Reading written instructions, whether or not the jurors receive a copy, does tend to make the judge's job easier. It becomes merely a matter of making sure that what the trial judge says follows language approved in prior appellate decisions. Whether the process of reading aloud conduces to juror understanding is, of course, quite another matter.

After the judge has finished, the lawyers receive an opportunity to record their objections to his failure to give any particular instruction which one or the other thinks he improperly omitted (or, as the case may be, improperly included). Given the importance of the jury charge in changing the law itself, meticulous concern for detail is entirely understandable.

Lawyers usually pay special attention here, because failure to call the judge's attention to an untoward omission or insertion *before* the jury begins deliberating normally precludes any right to claim error later. In fact, to preserve a potential appellate point, the objecting lawyer must actually tell the judge the language he wants used. This may seem like nit-picking. Why does it not suffice to tell the judge, "I object to Your

Honor's failure to give my Requested Instruction Number 5"? The problem has two aspects.

First, lawyers hate to cut options. They like to maximize the number of appellate pathways available to themselves and their clients. The fuzzier things are at important points in the trial, the greater the chance that after the trial the losing lawyer, combing through the record, will be able to find *something* on which to base an appeal.

Second, a request to add specific language to a set of instructions already delivered lends itself much better to accurate assessment if the judge hears the exact words the lawyer wants. Again, if we look at the appellate possibilities, it is fairer for the lawyer to *speak* the phrases he wants the judge to use, rather than merely referring the court to a flock of paragraph numbers.

The rule allowing post-instruction requests does not reflect a policy of giving the lawyers maximum opportunity to sow the seeds of a successful appeal. It aims, rather, to afford the judge every reasonable opportunity to second-guess *himself*, and thus to correct any error before it can affect the trial's outcome.

The necessarily legalistic tone of the dialogue, and the occasional sonority of reciting every word of a requested instruction can turn the after-charge colloquy into a fairly dull affair, particularly for you, because it normally takes place in whispers at the bench. Nonetheless, the boredom will be undoubtedly easier to tolerate than what follows.

You felt useless during most of the drama, vulnerable during cross-examination, and powerless during the closing arguments. Now comes unrelieved agony. Sweating out a jury verdict combines dread, hope, ennui, uncertainty, and abundant time to wonder what in your catalogue of prior sins ever damned you to this fate. The trouble is, you cannot know that fate until the jury returns; yet no one can ever predict that moment, because jurors do not operate on a schedule. Your only comfort comes from knowing that the other side shares your agony. Anyway, in most civil litigation, the deliberations do not last beyond one day, and almost never go into a third.

Incidentally, as you know, civil-case jurors are never locked up for deliberations.

A nationwide shift away from requiring a unanimous jury vote for a verdict (except in criminal cases), and the previously-mentioned trend in some places, including the federal courts, toward juries of six, instead of the traditional twelve, help speed the deliberative process. In any event, although you may feel your life is at stake, remember, jurors tend not to "freeze," "hang," or deadlock when deciding civil lawsuits, as they sometimes do in criminal cases.

Any stir from the jury room will provoke instant agitation in the corridors outside the courtroom, though the deliberations may be taking place on an entirely different floor of the courthouse. The speed with which the tremor affects everyone defies normal rules of physics or even metaphysics. Try to hold yourself in check when you feel the motion. Many times, what starts out sounding like a verdict turns out to be only a question: a request for a repetition of part of the charge or an answer to a point (unfortunately, not always a pertinent point) on which the jury seeks guidance.

The tension attendant upon any hint of jury activity can sometimes produce astonishing results. The late Charles Wyzanski, one of the greatest federal trial judges, once received word that the jury had a question. Counsel and the parties hastened to the courtroom; the jurors assembled solemnly in the jury box. An assistant United States marshal took from the jury foreperson the piece of paper on which, as usual, the jurors had written their question. The normal procedure calls for the judge to read it and, after conferring with the attorneys, to deliver his answer. Unfolding the scrap and immediately reading it aloud, Wyzanski magisterially shared the inquiry with his audience: "Three with cream and sugar. Five black . . ."

Ultimately, however, rumor turns to truth. The jury has indeed reached a decision. Now everybody—you, the plaintiff, the lawyers, the judge, the court reporter, the court clerk, and any by-sitters who may happen to be in the courtroom will watch as the jury rises in response to the inquiry: "Have you reached a verdict?" Some people say they can predict the

result by the way the foreperson does (or does not) look at the plaintiff (or the defendant). We tend to think that the intensified uncertainty of those last few seconds before all doubt forever vanishes merely emphasizes that no one can ever safely predict what a jury will think or do.

"What is your verdict?" says the clerk or the judge.

"We find . . ." says the foreperson.

The trial is over.

Appeals—When the End Is Only a Beginning

High among the benefits of settling cases is finality—as in *finis* and "finished." Unfortunately, if the parties have elected to continue battling, certainty of conclusion still eludes them, even after trial and verdict. *Parties*—in the plural. Whether a litigant emerges from the courtroom in the warm glow of vindication or in the clammy grip of condemnation, the case accompanies her, and so does the possibility of more litigation. What may have appeared to be the war's last battle may well turn out only to be an uneasy armistice.

Our legal system provides the higher courts at least one opportunity to review virtually every trial-level final performance. The appellate process, however, does not guarantee the verdict-loser a second chance.

Before a case can make its way up the winding stair of appellate procedure, it usually has to pause on a landing or two at the trial-court level. Generally, the losing lawyer asks the presiding judge either to set the verdict aside and enter judgment for the verdict-loser, or simply to allow a new trial. To succeed in either event, the motion needs more than the

moving party's outrage or the judge's distaste for the result. If the judge believes that the trial was fair, she will leave it undisturbed, despite minor legal errors which she may have committed, or even her own belief that the verdict should have gone differently.

The test is stringent. A motion for judgment notwithstanding the verdict stands no chance of success unless the losing side's lawyer can persuade the judge that she has erred so egregiously (in allowing or excluding evidence, in denying a motion for directed verdict, or in charging the jury) that reversal by the higher court is almost certain.

Sometimes the matter is plain. For example, perhaps the judge permitted the case to go to the jury even though no one testified that the doctor's performance failed to meet the applicable professional standard. Or maybe the plaintiff introduced no expert evidence that the malpractice caused the patient's injury. Either of these miscues would probably induce a judgment to enter for the verdict-losing defendant. Suppose, however, that the ground of the motion is that the judge, over objection, permitted an operating-room nurse to testify that she heard another doctor say that the neurosurgeon-defendant had "performed the operation in a completely successful way." That is inadmissible hearsay. Still, if the jury found for the defendant, is the error enough, by itself, to compel a new trial? Perhaps the plaintiff offered only weak evidence of negligence; or perhaps the defendant's expert testified so vigorously and persuasively that the judge firmly believes the tainted evidence did not produce the favorable verdict.

Before she can take away the victory, the judge has to conclude that, absent her mistake, the winner not only *might* have lost but *probably would* have done so.

The test for granting a new trial is somewhat looser, freeing the judicial discretion slightly. Here the judge can weigh all the evidence, take an overall view of the trial, and ask herself whether the verdict comported with justice. This does not make her a free agent, at liberty to substitute her idea of the proper result for the jury's. It does, however, permit her to act in the

rare instance of plain unfairness or a runaway jury.

Many times, in contemplating the new-trial question, the judge must also consider the size of the verdict. Whether she thinks the jury's number high or low is immaterial, unless it is so large or so small as to shock the judicial conscience. Even then, she does not grant a new trial outright, but simply affords the verdict-winner an option: Accept a diminution (or increase) in the amount of the judgment, or undergo a new trial. (Actually, in the federal courts, the judge, for constitutional reasons, cannot suggest *adding* to a verdict; she can, however, make *reduction* an alternative to a new trial.)

Allowance of a new trial is almost never directly appealable, because the second go-around may obviate any appeal at all; the verdict may satisfy all parties—or, rather, leave them equally unsatisfied; the case may even settle, now that everyone knows exactly what the other side has—or lacks.

You probably wonder why all this torture is necessary. Even before achieving the appellate level, the case has to undergo many procedural twists, full of what seem to you technicalities, reeking of the lamp and old dusty law books. Why do we have to go through all this, you ask? Could we not just dispense with courts, trial and appellate, altogether?

The sentiment is understandable; some lawyers share it— at least in part. Still, if we excused the judicial system from resolving questions of professional competence, who would do it? Common sense suggests that the public would never accept a panel of physicians as an alternative. After all, if you were suing an architect for botching your remodeling job, would you want a covey of architects ruling on the performance (or misperformance)?

Besides, even if we could get around the jury right inherent in federal and state constitutions, would physicians really *want* to give it up, particularly in light of the doctors' favorable win-loss ratio? Anyway, no matter what the type of basic dispute-resolving tribunal, some sort of regulatory appeal process is necessary, if only to make sure that the tribunal is following proper procedure.

In the American judicial system, the appellate remedy car-

ries distinct and strict limitations, which most people do not understand. The most important point is simply that the right to appeal does not automatically ensure a second chance for the party which lost at the trial. Appellate courts perform an exceptionally narrow function. They look almost exclusively at what the *judge* did.

Consequently, as we have mentioned, the areas likely to draw their attention are rulings admitting or excluding evidence; the content of the judge's jury charge; and the denial of a new trial. The appellant must first of all demonstrate that the judge committed some kind of legal error. In addition, she has to show that the judicial miscue affected a substantial right of the losing party. The object is to ensure a *fair* trial, not a *perfect* one. It is not at all unusual for an appellate court to conclude that the trial judge erred but that the error, although regrettable, does not warrant either reversing the result or giving the verdict-loser a second chance.

Of course, in deciding where to draw the line between *reversible* error on the one hand, and *harmless* error on the other, the appellate court necessarily cuts itself considerable slack. This is a calculus so inherently incapable of precise application, or reasonable definition, that even someone not concerned with the outcome might well believe that in any given case the distinction between the two types of error may seem to depend simply on whether the appellate court (or a majority of the judges deciding the matter) agrees with what lawyers call "the result below."

The actual appeals procedure may vary from state to state, but in general this is what you can expect:

Once the trial judge has decided any post-verdict motions, the loser has a brief period—thirty days is a popular number—to file a formal "notice of appeal." Normally, but not always, the party who drew the short end of the verdict is the appellant. We say "normally" because sometimes the plaintiff ostensibly wins but thinks the verdict inadequate, and appeals.

After filing the notice, the appellant orders the trial-court record (primarily the transcript of what occurred in the courtroom, plus the exhibits) and files a "brief," a frequently lengthy

disquisition on the law as applied to the events of the trial. Soon thereafter, the appellee (the verdict-winner) submits an opposing brief.

"Appellant" ("uh-*pell*-unt" or "uh-pell-*ahnt*") and "appell-ee" ("uh-pell-*ee*") refer to the parties themselves. Of course, it is their respective attorneys who do the actual work. In fact, the client, whether appellant or appellee, has less to do with the appellate process than with any other part of the entire case. Nonetheless, it is still *your* case, with *your* professional reputation at stake. You should certainly feel free to ask your lawyer to send you copies of all documents, especially the record and the briefs. Best limit your input, however, to pointing out typos and misspellings.

Because the appeal process concerns only issues of law, you will not have so close a working relationship with your appellate attorney as you did with your trial counsel. This will be true even if the latter handles the appeal, but in many firms a separate department takes over when a case crosses into appellate territory. Medicine is not the only profession where specialties abound.

Human nature tends to build psychic scar tissue around unpleasant wounds. Thus, by the time the appeal actually comes to court again—now before a panel of higher-level judges—you may well have pushed the whole unpleasant matter into your mental back yard. Then again, your interest may still be high, at least enough for you to want to follow the proceedings. If you wish, your lawyer will tell you when the court has scheduled argument, and you can take a seat in the spectator section. Unlike trial courts, appellate courts have the luxury of operating with virtual certainty as to the date, time, and duration of the proceedings before them. You can therefore be sure the case will come up precisely on schedule.

If you elect to attend, remember that appellate argument is generally dull. Unless the case involves a sensational crime or a matter of compelling public importance, even in the nearly forty states that allow the visual media full access the live, on-the-spot video cameras stay largely out of higher courts.

The simple truth is that, watching the average argument,

the nonlawyer onlooker will most likely react with instant, total, and continuing boredom. Indeed, "argument" itself is an obvious misnomer. One sees no lightning bolts of rhetoric, no voices raised in anguish, no dramatic gestures, no appeals (excuse the pun) to the listeners' emotions, no crackling, interruptive objections. The *mise en scène* will feature a "bench" of three or more justices (as appellate judges are usually titled). Some state supreme courts and the United States Supreme Court have up to nine justices; most intermediate appellate courts, including the federal Courts of Appeals, operate in panels of three; the most popular number for state supreme courts is seven.

The talking runs about fifteen to twenty minutes a side, appellant's counsel first, then appellee's. Actually, the lawyers do not speak for the full allotted time. The justices interrupt to ask questions, sharpen issues, explore consequences, and (occasionally) pose hypothetical situations to test the validity of one or another point an attorney may be pressing.

At times, the spectator may think that the lawyer is arguing not against her opponent, but against a particular judicial inquisitor or, if her luck is bad, the entire bench. In keeping with the idea that an appeal tests the correctness of what the trial judge did or failed to do, the thrust of the discussion has little to do with who should have won the trial.

At the close of the oral arguments, the judges do not immediately caucus, reach a decision, and emerge to announce the winner. An appellate court is not a jury. The opinion announcing the court's collective conclusion will not emerge for weeks, perhaps months. Even then, the matter may or may not end. If the tribunal is the highest court in the state, one can rest virtually assured it will go no further. Despite the frequent vow of trial-court losers to "take this all the way to the Supreme Court," in fact very few state-court civil matters, particularly state-court tort cases, ever get there. Our system of federalism gives the states, not the Congress or the federal courts, exclusive power to make the substantive rules governing those cases. It takes a claimed violation of a *federal* constitutional right to bring the case even within range of the

Supreme Court. State tort claims almost never involve such issues.

Beyond that, the Supreme Court's power to pick and choose among the hundreds of cases that losing lawyers seek to press means that, even if the matter started in a federal court, the odds against its making the judicial Big Show are prohibitively unfavorable. No matter that the trial took place in a United States district court, and the appeal in a federal circuit court of appeals; the case reaches the Supreme Court only if four justices agree the Court will hear it. Generally, ordinary civil cases (including actions alleging malpractice) do not raise the kind of state-national issues or differences of opinion between two federal appeals courts that draw the High Court's attention.

The one opportunity for further review of a state appellate decision remains in that state's judicial structure. If the court which heard the appeal was an intermediate court—that is, if the state's highest court has not yet considered the matter— the middle-stage loser (who may, of course, have been the winner at trial) may succeed in convincing the top-level judges to review what has happened so far. Chances for success in that lottery improve if the case raises either a legal point which the high court has not yet considered, or a question on which it wishes to change the existing governing principle.

From your standpoint as consumer, the natural history of the appeals process only emphasizes the uncertainty of predicting the end result of any law-related dispute, even after the jury has returned a verdict. Because the jury's decision is thus a mere first cut, cases sometimes settle while the appellate briefs are still in the word processors. Some appellate courts have even begun to institutionalize the settlement-before-appeal, and have established mechanisms to encourage the parties to mediate their disputes between the verdict and the argument on appeal.

A final discouraging caution. Not every case goes "upstairs." Quite often, the losing doctor's insurance carrier declines to press the matter further. Perhaps the trial judge made no mistakes likely to result in reversal, so that an appeal would

most probably merely waste time and money. Again, maybe the verdict, although disappointing, was sufficiently below the "exposure" to amount to a favorable settlement.

Finally, although the case may have raised a legal point of "first impression," something the appellate courts have not yet considered, the insurance company may not think that *this* particular case offers a suitable setting in which to seek a satisfactory ruling. Rather than chancing an unfavorable precedent, the company may prefer to await a more promising opportunity.

Some Thoughts on Prophylaxis

T his may seem an odd place to talk about avoiding diffi-
culty. After all, we have just taken you through a mal-
practice suit, from inception to appeal. Are we not a little late
with advice designed to prevent problems?

If you are reading the book only *after* assuming the litiga-
tory starring role, then we are indeed locking the door on an
empty barn. If, however, you have not yet found yourself in
the target, waiting until now to raise the question of risk-
avoidance makes a certain amount of sense. After all, in get-
ting this far, you probably have acquired not only a "feel" for
the technical and emotional currents of malpractice litigation,
but, more important, a conscious or unconscious desire—a
determination, really—never to find your name to the right
of a "versus" sign. To paraphrase Dr. Johnson's famous
observation, impending disaster wonderfully concentrates the
mind. Now that you know how unpleasant a litigant's lot will
be, perhaps *your* mind can more readily absorb strategies
enabling you never to suffer it.

A little frankness is very much in order here. Nothing we

could possibly write can save you from one variety of mal-
practice, plain old carelessness. Doctors, like lawyers and air-
line pilots, prefer to think of themselves as routinely
hypercareful people whose work habits simply do not permit
error.

The truth, however, is that most professionals—doctors,
lawyers, and judges included—fall into two classes: those who
have already made a mistake, and those who are going to make
one. Whether the error is serious or trivial, and whether,
whatever its magnitude, it entails serious consequences for
the person making it, are additional separate matters.

We start, then, by confessing freely that although ignoring
a sponge count, misreading an X-ray, garbling a history, and
just plain missing a diagnosis are all errors which should not
happen, this book cannot suggest ways to prevent them. Nor
will we deal further with the commonsense principle, funda-
mental to virtually every profession, of maintaining complete,
accurate, and *unaltered* records, covering, from its inception,
every aspect of the doctor-patient relationship.

Instead, we ask you to mull a two-step method for dealing,
not with the mistake, but with its nonmedical consequences.
Actually, the first step might be called a prequel to error,
something like anticipatory damage control.

Observations of cases in hospital and court, and discussions
with doctors and lawyers have given us the firm impression
that the physician's *attitude* toward the patient and the family
plays a significant role in determining whether an error will
engender litigation. We mean here not merely the attitude
after things have gone wrong (a subject we will touch on
shortly), but the relationship which the physician has estab-
lished from the very start of the doctor-patient collaboration.

"Bedside manner" is a term sufficiently old-fashioned to
warrant its return to the medical lexicon. Here it means some-
thing beyond a cheerful way of discussing painful topics. That
is, of course, part of the concept. More important, though, is
the idea of *relationship,* a kind of temporary partnership, in
which the patient comes to understand that the physician
regards him not as one more specimen on which to demon-

strate mastery of science, but as a collaborator in health recovery and, more important still, as a coequal personality.

The professional frame of mind which doctors necessarily adopt often causes them to present to the patient as omnicompetent, ominscient, unapproachable, and faintly obnoxious. One manifestation which illustrates the whole attitude is something we have discussed earlier, the frequent habit of addressing patients—even patients considerably older than the physician—by the first name, as though the patient were a child and the physician an all-knowing adult.

This role-definition in turn raises more difficulties. First, it tends to emphasize to the patient how helpless he is, how dependent upon the physician's skill and approval. Second, it fosters in the patient the idea that, because the doctor knows everything and can accomplish anything, the restoration of health is a certainty.

As to the first, no one, of whatever age, likes to feel dependent. Even the subtlest assertion of control can infect the doctor-patient nexus with tension and resentment. We might add that with a male-doctor–female-patient combination the strain magnifies. The same increased potential for difficulty exists when the patient is of a minority and the doctor is not.

Naturally, you wonder how a patient can possibly resent anyone, especially a physician, who is only trying to bring skill, judgment, and dedication to bear in restoring health. We respond by asking you to consider whether in your life's experience (not merely your medical experience) you have observed an invariable congruence of emotion and logic.

People's feelings do not always follow the dictates of reason. Indeed, in many situations which ostensibly should produce gratitude, or at least understanding, but instead foment anger, the patient is, at least on an emotional level, aware of the incongruity. The guilt, the sense of I'm-wrong-to-feel-this-way, can lead to an anger which may well turn against you. If and when something in the treatment does produce an unfortunate result, the patient's state of mind, thus preconditioned to blame the physician, offers receptive ground for the seed of a malpractice claim.

Equally pernicious is the idea of the physician's infallibility. American culture tends to venerate medical professionals. Think of the advertisements that rely on doctors as endorsers (even, in the not-so-distant past, for cigarettes). Think of the enormous popularity of the media medicos: Dr. Kildare, Rex Morgan, M.D., and Marcus Welby, M.D. (or, if you are old enough, of their radio precursor, Dr. Jim Brent). Think of "my son (or daughter) the doctor."

Although this veneration brings rewards, psychic and monetary, it also entails substantial risk. "In part," say a prominent neurosurgeon and the executive director of the American Association of Neurological Surgeons, "we are victims of our triumphs." If a patient believes that the doctor can cure all ills, then, when the doctor fails, the patient, by a kind of psychological rebound effect, comes to blame not the vagaries of fate but the hitherto omnipotent physician. Nobody likes to learn the claylike composition of an idol's feet.

Here again, logic takes second place to emotion. Any rational person knows that not every treatment works and that no physician cures every ailment. Nonetheless, to paraphrase Dr. Johnson again, hope triumphs over experience. Marcus Welby never blew a diagnosis; neither should you. In this case, the patient is like the Red Sox fan who, knowing that even Wade Boggs fails at the plate more than 60 percent of the time, nonetheless vociferously expects a hit from every at-bat.

As with the patient's feelings of helplessness, the emotion of disappointment can, in the stress resulting from an unfortunate medical result, render the patient more susceptible to the idea of a malpractice claim.

The point is simply that paying attention to the psychology of the doctor-patient relation *may* enable you in the future to deflect what one might call marginal claims. If, however, you stitch a ribbon retractor inside the wound, or tell a parent to put heat on a feverish child's tender belly, not even the most thoughtful and attentive bedside manner will or should save you from the lawsuit.

So far we have been talking about what one might call advance work, trying to immunize the patient, as it were, from

unthinking resort to forensic force. What can you do in the almost-too-late situation, the horrifying time when you realize not only that you have in fact erred, but that you must tell the patient about it?

The honest answer is, Not much. Your wisest course is that of humane intelligence coupled with intelligent humanity. Entirely apart from the self-flagellation that besets any physician who knows that his conduct has harmed, or even killed, the very person who came to him for care, you are torn between your natural instinct to comfort the afflicted and your acquired realization that anything you say can and will be used against you in a court of law.

In this delicate calculus, no one can prescribe the right words, or even the statement of choice. What follows, therefore, is nothing more than a catalogue of suggestions that you may wish to ponder.

It is probably neither wise nor necessary to make any statement in the nature of a *mea culpa*. Breast-beating and wailing at this stage are definitely counterproductive, for the patient (or family) and for you. Your listeners want to know: (1) Did something go wrong (a question which the circumstances sometimes immediately answer)? (2) What exactly happened? (3) What, if anything, can be done? (4) What are the chances of things' getting better (or worse)? (5) What are the long-term prospects?

Now, in considering what—and, equally important, how—one responds, it is well to realize that, *if* a lawsuit starts, the patient (or family) and her lawyer will learn absolutely everything worth knowing about your professional behavior. If you doubt this precept, reread what we had to say earlier on the subject of pretrial discovery.

It is smarter at this early stage to make a virtue of necessity, and not even attempt to gloss over, or (as the politicians say) put a "spin" on, let alone conceal, any unpleasant facts. If the patient died because the oxygen supply failed, say so. If the patient's toe turned gangrenous because the cast was too tight, say so. At least no one will ever be able to say of you, in court or out, "He was afraid to tell us the truth; he kept lying, right

from the start." And if you simply do not know the answer, say so.

Another proposition worth considering is that people usually deal better with simple statements of truth than with complicated explanations. So, even if you think—even if you *know*—that urinary incontinence is an unavoidable risk of the most precise prostate surgery, do not use this particular moment to set out your justification. (If you did not inform the patient *before* the operation, you are in a different variety of trouble.)

At the same time, you will do yourself serious harm if, for example, you try to brush off the mechanics of a fatal in-surgery cardiac arrest as (a) just one of those things; (b) something no lay person could understand; (c) a matter which you are not obliged to explain; or (d) all of the above. A plain explanation of what caused the complication will suffice. Again, if you do not know the answer, say so. *But* if you do know, beware the pit of "I'm really not able to say," or similar smarmy locutions. Depend on it: That answer will be juxtaposed with the testimony of one of the OR people that your first words when the crisis started were, "Who the hell shut down the O_2?" This demonstration that you knew all along will, needless to say, blow up at precisely the moment best calculated to disembowel you and your professional reputation.

"Can I safely say anything?" you are probably wondering, recalling our keep-silent advice in Chapter Two. There, we were looking at a litigational matrix. Here, the doctor-patient relationship still exists, and must predominate. Wisdom in this context starts with recognition of feelings, yours and your listener's. Feelings, after all, are something people cannot quarrel with; they exist. Moreover, recognizing another's feelings equates in a very real sense with recognizing the other's personality. In the world today, people strive for recognition. Not recognition in the sense of plaudits for accomplishment, but recognition of the self, distinction from the mass.

"I feel bad about what happened." "I know that you are feeling distressed and frightened." "I know that you are going through a lot of pain." These are all honest, direct statements that put the matter on a person-to-person basis. They tell the

listener that you and he share a common humanity. That they will probably not cause you any forensic difficulty later is only a side-effect. The important thing is that, even in a time of impending personal disaster, they enable you to see yourself, and to have others see you, as a healer thinking not only of himself, but of those who come to him for aid.

Although you may be facing the aftermath of an episode in which your inadvertence harmed your patient, at least now you are trying to make sure the situation grows no worse. *Primum non nocere.*

The Doctor as Witness

CHAPTER SEVENTEEN

Expert:
Why,
Who,
and What?

Evidence comes into court in different forms: oral testimony, photographs, X-ray plates, videotapes, and even occasionally medical instruments. Of all these, testimony is the most important, if for no other reason than that every other form of evidence depends, in the final analysis, on someone's talking about it in court, or, rather, talking it into court. The necessity for live testimony does not always occur to the casual onlooker, or, if the truth be known, to every lawyer. Documents (and other objects) do not walk into the record unaccompanied. Absent an agreement between the parties, they require a speaking witness to introduce them. Unless a *person* is prepared to vouch for the item, it does not become evidence. Until a live witness testifies that the X-ray depicts the plaintiff's right arm, it is merely an unexplained shadowgraph. Until someone testifies that the piece of metal in her hand is a Lotte's nail of the type inserted in the patient's left tibia, it is nothing but a curious artifact.

Whether she is introducing documents or exhibits, or testifying orally, the chief function of the speaking witness is to

131

put information before the trier of fact—that is, the jury or (if neither side has claimed a jury) a judge. This she does by recounting what she has seen, heard, tasted, smelled, or felt. Subject to obvious exceptions (very young children, for example, or the insane), the law regards her as competent to give us that information. How much or how little the trier of fact will believe the witness is, of course, another issue.

Strictly limiting a witness's testimonial competence to those matters within personal knowledge and recollection necessarily excludes her speaking about anything other than what she observed. Thus she must not draw inferences. She cannot, for example, say, "I wasn't there when Ms. Bright and the doctor talked about the operation. But I saw her later that afternoon and she was smiling and joking, so I figured the doc told her it would be very simple."

Nor can the average witness proffer speculation or surmise, at least as to matters not within the ordinary person's experience. Descriptions, even common-experience analogies, are acceptable. Thus a witness may certainly say, "She was bent over double and holding her belly, like she had a bad stomach ache." We do not, however, permit testimony as to technical detail. No lay witness could ever testify, "Her face was so red, I'm sure her blood pressure was over 190." Indeed, no judge would allow a layperson to tell the jury, "I looked at the X-ray plate and saw the fracture."

The rule is simple: The ordinary witness cannot state an opinion on any subject whose mastery requires training and experience. Who, then, may properly do so? What qualifies a witness to opine? In one word: expertise. Courts entertain opinions only from people who, by reason of learning and skill acquired over time, have developed specialized knowledge about a particular topic.

Emphasis here is on the expertise itself, not necessarily on how the witness has attained it. So long as the individual satisfies the judge that she has the required familiarity with the subject, the jury will hear her opinion. How much weight the jury gives that opinion is another matter entirely. We will have occasion to talk again about the difference between allowing

a witness to testify (a question of *admissibility* of evidence) and believing what she says (a question of *credibility*).

The initial issue—Does this person possess the background to qualify her as an expert?—rests solely with the judge. Normally, the party calling the individual starts the direct examination with a series of questions designed to elicit her education, training, experience, teaching credentials, professional associations, academic and other honors, and publication record. Lawyers encourage expert witnesses not to be modest about their achievements (naturally enough, many do not require much encouraging). The resultant horn-blowing can induce terminal ennui.

Opposing counsel will sometimes graciously concede that "Dr. Cutter is well known as a surgeon; we certainly agree that she is qualified as an expert in that field." Will the lawyer who originally called Dr. Cutter to the stand accept this concession in the interest of speeding the wheels of justice? Not very likely. "Thank you," she will say, "but we would like the jury to get a little better idea of Dr. Cutter's background." (Translation: "We don't want to leave the jury believing that this witness is somebody we picked up in a sandlot; especially because we know you will be calling Dr. Klugel, who teaches two afternoons a month at the local medical school and whom you will therefore keep calling 'Professor' throughout the trial."

This kind of jocularity, spoken and tacit, can chew up quite a bit of time, unless the judge steps in. Some judges, in fact, out of consideration for everybody, have taken to requiring the lawyer calling an expert (not only a medical expert, but *any* expert) to prepare twelve copies of the person's curriculum vitae, to be distributed to the jury as the witness limbers up her larynx. This greatly reduces the qualification time.

Whatever form the initial presentation takes, when it ends, some judges immediately permit the opposing lawyer to cross-examine the witness as to her qualifications. Others do not, but instead make their determination of expertise immediately, leaving cross-examination in due course (i.e., after the full direct examination) to bring out any gaps in the witness's qualifications and expertise.

The judge plays a sharply limited role. By determining that the witness is an expert, she is not at all giving some judicial seal of approval to the forthcoming testimony. Instead, she is merely permitting the testimony itself. She does not in any way grade the expert; this is strictly a pass/fail examination. The judge decides whether the individual meets *minimum* requirements, which most, but not all, do. To fail, the witness must demonstrate a virtual 100-percent absence of professional background. Of course, whether the jury chooses to credit all, none, or some of the barely qualified expert's utterances is exclusively up to the jurors.

Nonetheless, although the jury is supreme as to evaluating testimony, the judge receives broad discretion in qualifying the expert, or indeed in deciding what constitutes expertise. Remember: In this context, "expert" really does not carry its ordinary connotation—i.e., the highest level of specialized knowledge and competence. It is thus not at all uncommon for trial judges—with the approval of the pertinent appellate courts—to conclude that, for example, a physician specializing in, say, psychiatry may render an opinion in radiography. The essential is possession of a medical degree. Anything else, particularly the obvious incongruity, is a matter of *credibility*, to be hammered by the opposing lawyer.

Because the role of the expert is such a familiar one, we sometimes overlook the reason for its prevalence. Although minimalism is not a common virtue among trial lawyers, the wise litigator will whenever possible follow the advice of the canny Boston courtroom veteran who, whenever asked to recommend the name of "a good expert," would consistently answer, half in jest and full in earnest, "No one."

Unfortunately, a medical-malpractice suit so wraps the factual issues in science and technology that no lay jury could possibly understand the issues, much less resolve them, without considerable testimonial help. The expert thus must assume a role which every physician has probably played at one time or another: teacher. We speak now not merely of the full-time or clinical professor of medicine, but also of the resident helping to train the interne and, most important of all, the doctor

teaching the patient. The witness is a special kind of medical teacher; we will discuss the testimonial educator in much greater detail later on.

A doctor-witness fills one other important function. Like anyone taking the stand, she is there because the lawyer calling her believes the evidence will help the attorney win the case for the client. This is certainly true for the *percipient* witness—i.e., someone who has information useful to a decision, as, for instance, a bystander who happened to observe an accident, or a physician who treated the plaintiff. It is even more true for an expert witness, whose participation, after all, has been bought and paid for.

Notice that we said "participation," not "testimony." Although many lay people, and, unfortunately, many lawyers, regard the expert as a "hired gun" whose motto is "Have mouth, will testify," any good expert (which is to say, any effective expert) takes pay not for her opinion, but for her time and her expertise. Is this universally true? Certainly not. Can one find people with qualifications sufficient to rate them as experts who will produce whatever opinion may be required by whichever side first retains their services? Unfortunately, yes. Some of them are even physicians, doctors who, as Judge Charles Wyzanski once remarked in open court, spend more time testifying than treating.

The presence of these doctors does not, however, change this basic precept: The test of a physician's courtroom effectiveness is not willingness to please her sponsor but, rather, (1) whether she knows what she is talking about; and (2) whether she is able to communicate that information to the jury. By combining these two vital attributes, a doctor-witness necessarily and properly transcends the role of mere purveyor of medical opinion, and inescapably becomes in the best sense an advocate, a contributing member of the litigation team. Bear in mind, though, that advocacy of this kind depends for effect on invisibility; blatancy destroys credibility or, worse, turns the argument against its proponent.

CHAPTER EIGHTEEN

This Mind for Hire?

In the last chapter, we used the phrase "hired gun" when discussing the layperson's conception of an expert witness. The term and the idea it embodies have wide currency. Because juries consist almost entirely of people not conversant with the expert's field, whatever it may be, this understanding— or, rather, misunderstanding—can seriously influence the jurors' collective ability to reach a just verdict. Any expert witness must both recognize the prejudice and allow for it.

The contempt for experts—any and all experts, as a class— proceeds from the inherent uncertainty of almost every scientific statement. This is particularly true in medicine. Of course, one can easily recite numerous incontestable facts: Decapitation invariably entails death; amputated limbs do not regenerate; the body needs oxygen for life. Yet at the fringes, so to speak, of many such apparent certainties, one often finds curious exceptions, which disturb the heretofore easy assurance of scientific verity. For example, although the physics of falling from a great height apparently guarantee trauma suf-

ficient to produce inescapable death, people have in fact been known to survive just such an experience. Similarly, notwithstanding the easily demonstrable fatality of remaining underwater beyond a very brief time span, individuals occasionally come out of, say, a five-minute total immersion without any ill-effect at all. Whether we call these extremely rare occurrences miracles or simple statistical aberrations, we have to admit that sometimes they do happen. An exception may merely prove a general rule, yet its rarity does not destroy the event's own independent significance.

The line between can-never-happen and might-possibly-happen or even infinitesimally-likely-to-happen is neither unfailingly clear nor predictably bright. Drawing the line therefore becomes a matter of debate—a one-sided debate in many instances, but still a debate. You may remember what a doctor named Arthur Conan Doyle wrote: "When you have eliminated the impossible, whatever remains, however improbable, must be the truth." The inescapable corollary of that principle is that at times the improbable may indeed *be* the truth.

If one can find room for differences of opinion about such apparently unarguable premises as the certainty of death after long submersion, how much more likely to spawn dispute are matters in which the *science* of medicine takes second place to the medical *art*—diagnosis, surgical technique, dosage, and treatment regimen?

Because within any allegation of medical malpractice smolders a disagreement over the art of medicine (as the defendant employed it), the issue must depend for its resolution by a lay group—the jury—on presentation by one or more experts. The nature of the dispute, moreover, ensures that each side will offer expert testimony.

Thus we are certain to have at least two opposed experts. Now, it is a fact of human nature that, when someone expresses an opinion, the act of expression tends itself to confirm the opiner in the validity of that view. This phenomenon occurs most obviously when the opinion rests on the propounder's

own fund of experience and knowledge. It flares with special brilliance when someone of comparable background takes a contrary view.

Whether practitioner, academic, or layperson, we all react adversely to anyone pressing an opinion differing from our own. In the context of litigation, an expert quickly sheds the scientist's desideratum (rare enough under the best circumstances): Doubt your own conclusions and cheerfully invite someone else to point out any deficiencies of observation, technique, or reasoning which may have flawed the path to your present position.

When operating the way it is supposed to, the adversary-expert system presents to the trier of fact the informed, opposed views of two individuals, each of whom has followed a psychological trajectory which started with a determination based on analysis of the facts, continued through an association with the litigational position of the party who first sought the expert's opinion, and culminated in a direct competition with the opponent's expert.

We readily concede that this paradigm does not cover all cases and all experts. Certainly some testifying professionals maintain detachment and eschew partisanship. Given the inherently competitive nature of litigation, however, and the attorney's obligation to obtain and present the evidence most favorable to his client's position, it is not surprising that when a consultant gives, for whatever reason, an unfavorable opinion, the lawyer turns to someone else, or at least tries to find another savant. On the other hand, as we have suggested, once his view causes a party to retain him, even the most neutral expert will to a greater or lesser extent perceptibly become a partisan, doing his best to ensure that *his* side wins.

Just as many experts approach the task with open minds, becoming active, striving members of the team only later in the litigation, some qualified experts turn the process inside out. They reason from conclusion to premise, asking or perceiving what the desired opinion is, and then undertaking to give it. We cannot deny that such individuals exist; in our

experience, they constitute a minority among expert witnesses.

Although a current popular view holds that experts are (like the lawyers who obtain their testimony) nothing but mercenaries, available at a price to whoever is willing to pay for their services, we urge the distinction between, on the one hand, prostitution of the intellect and, on the other, the competitiveness engendered by a vigorous belief that one's professional views are not only correct, but exclusively so. Failure to draw the distinction may lead to an emotional belittling of the other side's expert and, even worse, to an inaccurate appraisal of unfavorable expert testimony. That, in turn, can produce an erroneous evaluation of one's own litigational position.

We need hardly add that, in the courtroom as in the operating room, when it comes to assessing the situation and preparing a plan of action, emotion is almost always a fatal contaminant of clear thought. Better, therefore, to take the expert on his own terms, as someone honestly (if mistakenly) holding a contrary opinion. Attack the opinion, but leave out of the dispute the individual who espouses it.

CHAPTER NINETEEN

The Fee Simple

When an expert comes under cross-examination, one can gauge the interrogating attorney's depth of experience by whether or not she asks this question: "Doctor, how much are you being paid for your testimony?" Any moderately sophisticated witness will calmly reply, "Nothing."

If the inquisitor is an eager tyro, she will expostulate, "You mean you want this jury to believe that you're receiving nothing for your opinion?" Comes the answer: "I am not being paid for my evidence; I am being paid for my time."

The difference is neither pedagogic nor trivial. Although the clumsy attorney hopes the jury will conclude that the witness offers whatever opinion the side employing her wants delivered, in fact, as we have said, it is not the opinion itself, but the expert's willingness to give it, which warrants recompense.

An expert who testifies at a trial is rendering a service. We denigrate neither her personality, her professionalism, nor her skill by comparing her, in that respect, to anyone whose training and experience enable her to perform a function and to

be paid for doing so. A suggestion that the payment somehow taints the service carries no more moral or ethical validity than a contention that a physician should not charge a fee for providing medical care.

Any expert witness, but particularly a physician, must come prepared to explain her full connection with the case. If, for example, she has spent hours examining records, refreshing her understanding by library research, and physically examining the plaintiff, she increases her effectiveness (as a witness) by furnishing the details to the jury. Of course, if she has not invested much time, the paucity of her preparation most probably will weaken her evidence, especially if she is to receive a flat fee which, divided by the scant number of hours, produces a large dollars-per-hour figure.

The question of time is always delicate. Five minutes of X's thought may be worth vastly more than two hours of Z's, but the average juror is likely to have an opposite initial reaction. Beyond that, an opinion reached after only a brief time carries the flavor of haste or (worse) of a predisposed mind.

In any event, one must make the jury understand that the opinion, however speedily derived, is the result not of snap judgment but, rather, of clear thinking based on experience. Probably the best way to do this is to share your reasoning process with the fact finder. Take advantage of the trial structure: You speak first, because direct examination precedes cross; thus you and the lawyer who has retained you have a chance to shape the dialogue even before the enemy can get you in range.

When you hold your final pretrial conference with the lawyer who is calling you as a witness, be sure she knows to frame her questions so as to allow you to present both your reasoning *and* your conclusion. The order does not matter, and may well depend upon the subject. Sometimes the more effective exposition comes from stating the conclusion, then giving the supporting reasons. In other contexts, you may be better off building to a conclusory climax. The attorney's trial strategy, of course, will play a significant part in the planning. She will welcome your input, or at least tolerate it; but only she can

make the final strategic and tactical decisions, including the manner and order in which she will present the evidence, yours and everyone else's.

When getting ready for the witness stand, an expert must always remember that wise counsel do not attack conclusions or reasoning head-on. Experienced lawyers realize that, although they may score an occasional point, they cannot hope to match, in her own field, someone who has devoted a professional lifetime to mastering a difficult and technical area of knowledge.

Instead, they seek to pick away at smaller matters, hoping to dull the expert's gloss, and perhaps to persuade the jury that, if the witness trips on one or two small matters, she cannot be very surefooted on larger ones. If along the way the lawyer can score a substantive hit or two, so much the better; she counts that, however, as pure gravy.

One such trick aims to emphasize the mouth-for-hire characteristic that many people—including doctors—associate with expert witnesses. "Tell us, doctor, if you will, just how many times you have testified in the past two years." The idea, of course, is to show that the physician spends so much time in court that she is, figuratively, more of a trial participant than a doctor.

The late San Francisco thoracic surgeon Harold H. Lindner used to dilute the effect of this ploy by pulling out a pocket notebook and reading the exact number into the record. If the lawyer was foolish enough to ask the question which often follows the how-many-court-appearances inquiry (i.e., "And you most often testify for defendants [plaintiffs], don't you?"), Dr. Lindner would say,"Well, actually, according to my record. . . ," and then read the score aloud. Because the figure demonstrated a fairly even split, the attorney would usually turn to other pastures.

Not every witness's testimonial track record permits her to use this gambit. The best response, therefore, is, as always, the honest one. If you have indeed testified eighteen times in the past six months, always for the defendant, say so. Respond promptly, directly, cheerfully (but not in a clownish manner),

and without embarrassment. Let your manner convey your sincerity. Do not try to turn the question back on the interrogator. By training, experience, and disposition, she is far better equipped than you to get the best of that duel.

Sometimes an expert will almost certainly appear vulnerable to an accusation of testimony-for-hire. Suppose, for instance, you are in the position we mentioned before of having examined the plaintiff only briefly. If you are testifying for the defendant, you may have met the plaintiff only once, when she appeared at your office, accompanied by her attorney, to submit to a physical examination as ordered by the court, or as agreed by the lawyers. You conducted the examination, reviewed whatever medical or hospital records were made available to you, and wrote the report which you submitted to the defendant's attorney. All perfectly appropriate and normal.

The jurors, though, may view it differently. They may wonder how a short exposure to the plaintiff and her condition can possibly give you enough information to form a meaningful opinion. This natural doubt in turn furnishes the opposing attorney with ammunition for significant impeachment. She will try to leave the jurors with the impression that you came to the examination with a mind already predisposed. She will suggest, first by questions, then during closing argument, that the examination was a sham, and that your testimony does not merit the jurors' trust or even attention.

This scenario plays with still greater effect if you happen to be an expert testifying for the plaintiff, and part of the basis for your opinion is an examination conducted in the courthouse. Never happens, you say? Believe us, it does. If, for example, the case involves an issue as to the plaintiff's range of mobility, and you have brought your knowledge up to date by checking her progress with a simple examination just outside the courtroom, the attorney will doubtless ask whether you normally conduct your medical practice in corridors of public buildings.

In either of these situations, the attorney wants to ignite the hired-gun prejudice. Frankly, you cannot do much to parry

the thrust. Once again, the principle is *primum non nocere*. Your best bet—or, more accurately, your least bad strategy—is to accept reality and to avoid any appearance of evasion. The time in which, or the place where, you conducted the examination is a given. You will only look foolish trying to slide over or minimize the facts. Better to tell the jury straight out that you took whatever time was necessary to obtain the facts that you thought necessary to provide you with the basis for a medically sound conclusion. "I conducted an examination in my office to the fullest degree that the case required," or "You can adequately determine the range of motion of a person's arm just about anywhere." Once again, we urge, do not fence with the questioner. Make your point in the most matter-of-fact manner possible, and calmly await the next question.

The Witness as Teacher: Making Contact

When considering ways to improve your performance and effectiveness as an expert witness, start by focusing on *why* and *how* the law allows expert testimony in the first place. As we mentioned in Chapter Seventeen, the courts permit someone with skill and experience to render an opinion on matters within his field of expertise. They do so, however, when and only when the subject of the testimony is something that the average juror could not be expected to deal with on the basis of his own experience.

This limitation, never forget, has two effects, one mandatory, the other exclusory. To take a simple, nonmedical example, a jury would need expert assistance before being able to decide whether a particular brake drum was so worn down that it lacked the physical capacity to stop the car. The jury would not, however, hear expert testimony as to whether, after the defendant had for some weeks noticed difficulty in stopping the car, he was negligent for failing to have a mechanic diagnose the condition and repair it.

Similarly, the jury *must* have expert testimony about the risks

normally associated with a particular surgical procedure. But in deciding whether or not the physician informed the patient of those risks, and whether or not a reasonably careful physician would have done so, the jury relies on its own understanding of the circumstances, in accordance with the judge's instructions as to what the law requires the plaintiff to prove.

Of course, the boundary between expert-required and expert-excluded is neither sharp nor inveterate. In many situations, the choice lies entirely in the judge's discretion (thus making prediction risky), or in the appellate court's determination (negating prognostication severely). Nonetheless, at the trial-court level, the rule results in a clear imperative to every expert witness:

You are in court only to explain to the jurors something that without your testimony they could not understand. Therefore, whatever your profession, whatever the extent of your academic experience, *you are now a teacher.* Furthermore, whether you are used to teaching medical students, residents, or postdoctoral fellows, your class now consists of that small group in the jury box, a group representing the lay community. (We defer for a moment considering the courtroom class with only one student, and that one wearing a black robe, the judge-tried case.)

The principles which govern the art and science of teaching apply with equal force no matter what the instructional context. Although it is not necessarily true that a good teacher makes a good witness, courtroom observation demonstrates daily that *every* good expert witness is a good teacher. If you have not testified before, you may wish to read (or reread, if you are fortunate enough to have discovered it already) Gilbert Highet's wise, subtle, and unpretentious distillation of wisdom, *The Art of Teaching.* Of course, Professor Highet had in mind the small classroom and the lecture hall, not the courtroom. Nonetheless, his book furnishes more usable suggestions on the essence of the teacher's (or expert's) function than many a text aimed solely at the witness box.

An expert comes to the stand for the single purpose of instructing the jurors in matters which they cannot otherwise

be expected to understand. His only aim, therefore, is to impart information. Everything else must necessarily subordinate itself to that end; conversely, everything the witness does while testifying—everything—must justify itself in terms of the goal.

Now, "conveying information" is really just another definition of the currently much-overused word "communicating." Before you can inform another person—that is, give him facts or ideas which he can use—you must get through to him. This is a concept ludicrous in its simplicity; yet, over and over, witnesses, skilled and learned though they may be, and, of course, many teachers, from nursery school to graduate school, ignore it completely. They forget that adequate reception must precede comprehension.

The witness thus must be able to take in the words you speak. A witness who mumbles or adopts erratic speech rhythms will never reach the listener's mind. When radio interference fouled the reception, all of Churchill's eloquence became nothing more than static.

No matter how cogent, clear, and concise a witness's thought, no matter how accurate the science behind it, the failure to articulate and enunciate will cut off communication as effectively as a physical gag. The net effect, in fact, is even more unfortunate. Watching someone physically restrained from speaking, the observer at least recognizes that an outside force, not the would-be speaker, prevents the transmission. When a witness whispers or cloaks his words with nervous coughs or distracting mannerisms, the listener unconsciously comes to conclude that the speaker either deliberately wishes to remain mysterious, or that he so lacks belief in his thoughts that he hesitates to express them. In either event, confusion turns to frustration, and then to hostility. Thus any subsequent statement which may miraculously emerge through the fog will meet total rejection.

The first essential of testifying, then, is acquiring a delivery format which ensures hearers' understanding. If you have any doubt about your accomplishments in this regard, do not wait until the trial to check yourself out.

Instead, go through a practice run, using a tape recorder.

Ask the lawyer to write out some of the questions he is likely to pose during your direct examination at the trial. Have a friend or your spouse read the questions to you while you respond, with the tape running, in as natural a manner as possible. If for whatever reason you crave privacy, go off by yourself, read each question, and then answer it aloud.

Remember, the purpose here is not to polish your form but, rather, to get the most honest and accurate appraisal of your communication skills. So just answer the questions with only the thought necessary to frame the substance; do not use the exercise to *rehearse* your future courtroom performance.

Once you complete your run-through, put the tape aside for a day or so. Then, at a quiet time, go off somewhere and play it back. Be warned: Hearing your recorded voice is usually an unnerving experience. "Ugh," is the most gentle response. "Do I really sound that bad?" This natural repugnance comes from the shock of realizing that the voice you hear yourself using every day is not the everyday voice the world hears coming out of your mouth. You hear the sound of your own voice as it resonates through your bony structures; your listener hears it straight from your larynx.

Concentrate on what the tape tells you. Is the voice understandable? Are the individual words clear? Does an idiosyncratic cadence or an irregular modulation (especially lowering the voice at the end of sentences) make your thought difficult to follow? Can *you* understand the taped message? For an even better test, if you feel up to it, give the tape to your spouse or a close friend (or the lawyer who has retained you). Ask for a candid response to the same questions we have suggested that you ask yourself.

A final step in this phase of your preparation is the verbal equivalent of a road test. With the lawyer's cooperation, find out when the courtroom where the trial will take place is going to be vacant and go there. Get a "feel" for the acoustics. Find out if the layout includes an amplifying system. If it does not, have a friend sit in the jury box while you speak from the witness box. Does your voice carry adequately? If at trial the jurors are constantly indicating that they cannot hear you, or

if the judge feels obliged to interrupt your testimony with constant requests ("Doctor, would you please speak a little louder?"), the force of your evidence dies with a whimper. Experts who speak in hushed tones do not generally win cases.

You do not have to become a professional lecturer or stand-up performer to give effective testimony. You do, however, have to make yourself understood.

Although vocal clarity is an absolute essential to successful communication, impeccable diction is not a guarantee that your listeners are getting your message. If your modulated tones convey unintelligible jargon, you might as well testify in pantomime. To reach the listeners, you must speak their language.

Sounds simple and obvious, does it not? You probably think of yourself, with good reason, as easy to understand, whether speaking to a patient, a colleague, or a casual acquaintance. Whatever the situation, be it personal conversation or broad-gauge presentation, you believe firmly that no one has any difficulty grasping your meaning.

Without denigrating your command of English, and without condescension toward the people who serve as jurors, we think it essential for you to understand that when you speak from the witness box, you will be facing an audience that does not necessarily share your outlook or your vocabulary. Furthermore, none of your listeners will be able to ask you to explain, as any casual conversation partner, certainly any co-professional, and even the judge sitting without a jury would do.

You must therefore choose a vocabulary that your audience will understand, even if that choice forces you to abandon the scientifically "correct" word in favor of the unprofessional, inexact lay term. You are not, after all, trying to demonstrate the extent of your medical vocabulary. Nobody will grade you down for using slang. Quite the contrary: The jurors may administer a thundering flunk if your otherwise impeccable word-selection fails to let them know what you are talking about.

From medical school—perhaps even from premed days—

physicians have prided themselves on using *the* technically accurate term. Ordinary folk talk about the elbow bone; the physician calls it the "olecranon." The vocabulary almost defines the professional. Admittedly, common usage may sometimes cause real difficulty or confusion. The layman's "stomach ache," for example, can connote a gamut of pain, from the simple muscle pull to an incipient ulcer. So, medically speaking, terminological exactitude is not an affectation, but a necessary tool for the physician in helping the patient.

In court, the witness has an entirely different goal: making the jurors understand. Nothing else. Aiming at any other target likens the witness to a physician who sutures the gashed leg beautifully but neglects to reduce the underlying fracture. When you testify, you must severely crop your technical vocabulary, if you cannot temporarily forget it entirely. In this regard, the best advice we can give is: Use the least possible amount of medical language, just enough to get your point across.

Obviously, you should use the ordinary word, rather than the scientific equivalent, unless doing so will lead you into a misstatement. As a good rule of thumb, never use a Latin term, or, indeed, any foreign word. Eschew foreign pronunciations, as, for example, "sahn-tee-meter" instead of "sen-tuh-meter." Avoid shorthand expressions, no matter how elementary a physician would find them. Do not say "McBurney's point," nor even define it as "A point on the abdominal wall located by placing the thumb on the navel and the middle finger on the iliac crest, then dropping the index finger." Instead, say, "A place on your abdomen about halfway between your belly button and your hip bone."

If you absolutely must use a technical term, define it immediately, using simple, easily understood language: "We inserted a Lotte's nail. That's a three-sided piece of steel, about a foot long, that goes inside a fractured leg bone to bridge the break and to keep the leg strong and solid."

Remember at all times that some words which have a perfectly common *medical* definition also mean something quite different to the average juror (or judge, for that matter). You

can shock and confuse the audience you are supposed to be teaching if you stud your testimony with gems like "toilet," "irrigation," "tolerate," "insult," "fix," "compromise," and "portal." Even "venous" slipped casually into a sentence can set a *listening* juror to images of an armless goddess.

You can almost always express the medical meaning in lay language easily enough, and thus avoid difficulty. The trouble is that, like any technical term peculiar to any profession, the arcane word, by shortening expression, saves time and (most important) mental effort. The temptation becomes ingrained, and irresistible. Avoiding these buzzwords is nonetheless essential. Give the task considerable attention and effort, not only while you testify but before you go to court.

Beyond reliance on technical lingo, physicians tend to fall into certain locutions which end up isolating them from their audience. The best example is the almost invariable tendency to use "one" as a personal pronoun in situations where the ordinary person would say "you" or "I," or even "we": "One tries to avoid exposing the phrenic nerve," or "One would ordinarily not prescribe Demerol," or "One expects one's patient to report change."

Grammatically, this is all perfectly proper and correct. And if one were delivering a paper at a colloquium, one's peers would doubtless approve one's syntax. Unfortunately, if one talks this way to jurors, one cannot avoid an aura of condescension and supercilious snobbery, and certainly a distancing of oneself from whoever it is one seeks to influence. This is true, by the way, whether the target is twelve jurors or one judge.

One can easily test the point: Read the preceding paragraph aloud twice, once as written, the second time substituting "you" or "your" as appropriate. Which sounds better? Which sounds more the way people normally talk? Ask a lay friend to perform the test. Which does he find more attractive? When you listen to him, which mode most appeals to you?

Whatever aspect of verbal communication one considers (or, rather, you consider), we say again, the expert witness, as

teacher, has a single purpose: teaching. In this context, teaching means explaining. It means taking a subject that by definition is something far removed from the average person's field of knowledge and experience, reducing it to understandable terms, and then communicating it so that the listener knows what you are talking about.

Up to now, we have focused on the means of communication, the verbal tools. Now we examine some of the techniques for ensuring that those you are supposed to be teaching will indeed learn the necessary lesson.

The Witness as Teacher: Making Your Point

So far, we have been concentrating on your style, the means by which you deliver your ideas to your listener. Now let's focus on the substance of your communications.

For this purpose, we assume that, by whatever means, you have developed a courtroom manner which permits you to talk to the jurors in a way calculated to put them at ease, or at least not to put them off. We assume also that your choice of words informs, rather than mystifies. In short, we assume that you and the jury are, figuratively and literally, eye to eye and mind to mind.

You have now reached the essence of your role as an expert witness: teaching the jurors what they need to know. The task is not easy, but observing a few commonsense principles—some of which we have already mentioned—can make success much more likely. "Success" in this context means, of course, that when you finish testifying your efforts will have brought the jurors to an understanding of whatever points you have been retained to impart.

We emphasize this fairly obvious conclusion because many

expert witnesses, some from distinguished academic back-
grounds, do not appreciate that jury comprehension is not
the most important goal; it is the *only* goal. Achieve that, and
nothing else matters; fail to attain it, and nothing will vindi-
cate you. You must therefore make certain that you apply to
your behavior, demeanor, and performance a standard befit-
ting the immediate necessity you face.

This means constantly reminding yourself that your audi-
ence consists of people from diverse backgrounds which do
not ordinarily include medicine, or even science. These are
not your professional colleagues, or a certifying board, or res-
idents, or students. Moreover, although the average juror is
content to perform jury service, and generally tries to fill the
role conscientiously and competently, the trial is necessarily
of secondary concern. Thus, unlike the students who are pay-
ing to hear you, or the colleagues and examiners to whom
your utterances are an important and desired professional
event, the jury is attending involuntarily. Captive audiences
do not always contain enthralled listeners.

One other significant circumstance differentiates jurors from
the groups to whom you generally demonstrate your medical
proficiency and knowledge: Ordinarily, the jury cannot ask
questions; you will receive no verbal "feedback" about your
pacing, emphasis, or recapitulation. In fact, because jurors
instinctively try for the poker-faced response, do not count
on body language to bridge the communications gap. Even in
a judge-tried case, where questioning is much more likely, the
black-robed solitary auditor may prefer—as many judges do—
to take the evidence as it comes, whatever the indigestible form.

This lack of response, added to the constraints imposed by
the courtroom question-and-answer format, to say nothing of
the rules of evidence, can cramp your style and distort your
performance. We will have some suggestions for ameliorating
the difficulty, but you ought to bear it in mind from the start.

More truly than in any other teaching milieu, instructional
success here depends on the Three C's:

Conciseness. You must reach the heart of the matter quickly;
if you have a number of points, you must reach each one

without delay. Even in complicated matters, avoid circumlocution or prolixity.

Clarity. You must plan what you have to say so that the information flows smoothly and logically, always keeping in mind that your audience knows a good deal less than you do about your subject—and about medicine generally.

Comprehension. You must subordinate everything to that single great end, the jury's understanding.

The need for conciseness springs from a demonstrable trait in the American character: a short attention span. Fostered by the episodic nature of any television drama (to suit the need for commercial intervals) and television's devotion to the thirty-second sound bite, the national desire for quick results generates a mind-set highly intolerant of anything even remotely resembling delay. Whether one lauds the trait or deplores it, failure to account for it can cost a speaker her audience or a teacher her class. Americans expect from every instructor entertainment as well as enlightenment, in no less than equal proportions. Today's quintessential pedagogic sin is "borrrrring" the listener.

A witness-teacher must therefore always sharply focus her presentation. She must speak in short sentences, putting her thoughts in the fewest number of words necessary to express her meaning. This kind of delivery does not always come naturally. Often it requires conscious preparation and thought. At a minimum it demands constant effort to hear yourself with others' ears, and to know, before beginning a sentence, pretty well where (and how) it will end.

You will have only a limited time to make your point. The rules of evidence, the attention span of the jurors, and the natural tendency of overburdened judges to urge dispatch, all combine to preclude any kind of lengthy background-filled discourse. In travel, getting there may be half the fun; in testimony, arriving is the whole exercise.

You must plan in advance not only what you will say and the way you will say it, but how you can convey the maximum amount of information in a manner that allows your lay listeners to follow you effortlessly. Of course, you cannot arrange

this presentation on your own. The introduction of direct evidence (as opposed to cross-examination) is a duet, not a solo performance.

Indeed, the choreography of testimony itself demands a team effort. You have the scientific information, but the lawyer is the forensic specialist. It is she who understands (a) laying out a chain of evidence to produce maximum effect; and (b) the procedural rules which control the kind of information that she and you can present.

You have a right to know just what the lawyer expects from you by way of evidence. She has an equal right to know precisely what your testimony will disclose. To this end, it is essential that you and the lawyer who has retained you confer, in person if possible, but at least by telephone, if time or geography will not permit a face-to-face meeting.

You must not hesitate to ask for such a conference if the lawyer fails to do so. Sadly enough, experience suggests that many attorneys content themselves with only a cursory preparation; instead, they rely on the expert to "do her stuff," virtually as a matter of rote.

Make certain that you and the lawyer go over your prospective testimony thoroughly. Of course, any but the most incompetent of attorneys will at least talk with her expert. That is not what we mean. A hasty "I'll-ask-you-this-and-you'll-answer-thus" does not constitute adequate preparation.

To do the job right, you and the lawyer must undertake to teach each other. For your part, you must tell her what you mean to say; you must explain the significance of what you will testify; and you must make sure she understands both the testimony and its pertinence. Do not be afraid to go over points which may seem obvious to you; do not assume that the attorney, no matter how much experience she may have had in trying cases, even cases involving medical evidence, knows as much as you. Dig unabashedly into the tedious detail. If the lawyer thinks she has heard enough, she will certainly tell you.

On the other hand, never forget that one characteristic of a good trial lawyer is the ability to soak up knowledge quickly. Of course, the nature of the profession means that she will

not keep the expertise for very long. Nonetheless, for whatever time may be necessary—that is, during the preparation period and the trial—she will retain the knowledge to a degree that will surprise you—and will enable her to discuss the subject with you on a fairly elevated plane.

The lawyer, if she is doing the job right, should explain to you the framework of questioning, the way any particular evidentiary rules may affect what she asks and what you are permitted to answer. She will also go over with you the pitfalls that cross-examination may present. Here you can help greatly. If your position is scientifically or factually vulnerable, this is the time to let her know. Forewarned, she may be able to minimize the damage by bringing the bad news out during your direct examination, instead of waiting for the other side to detonate it during cross-examination.

How intense should the preparation be? Although the answer depends on the case, a good general rule is simply this: You and the lawyer must work out a plan which will ensure the jurors' receiving *all* the information they need in a format that will make the point as plainly as possible, and therefore with minimum clutter.

A good direct examination of an expert witness—or, for that matter, of any witness—should seem effortless, proceeding with elegant clarity to a conclusion which in retrospect appears obvious. We need hardly remind you that in this, as in many performances, from conducting a symphony orchestra to removing a gallbladder, what the observer sees as easy, smooth, and natural requires immense preparation. Only through effort can a performance appear effortless.

Remember, however, not to confuse preparation and understanding one's place in the team with rehearsal, still less with script memorization. It is one thing to be certain—and to make counsel certain—of what you will bring into evidence. It is quite something else to attempt exact prediction, and something worse to establish in advance the precise phraseology. In most cases, direct examination seems to work best when counsel and you have a general albeit thorough understanding of what she will ask and you will respond. If some

specific, narrow points are essential, then of course you should be ready to make them, and to let counsel know exactly how you will state them. For the rest, a broader orientation suffices. You do not want to give the jury an impression of rote learning. Once again, recall that you are a teacher, and that no good teacher ever drones the content of a lesson.

Now, with the background preparation accomplished, you are almost ready for the actual class and the live students. The remaining pretrial suggestion concerns your appearance. We urged in Chapter Eight that a doctor's courtroom clothing should match the community's expectations. This is as true for the disinterested witness as for the litigant. Fail to fit the pattern—call it a couturial stereotype if you wish—and the jury will focus more on your tailoring than your testimony. If you are planning to testify in a court away from your home base, ask the lawyer *before you pack your suitcase* what garb is appropriate. When you step to the stand, let your audience be all ears, not all eyes.

We have suggested this before, but it merits repetition and re-emphasis: Effective testimony rests upon explanation, not expostulation. Your job is to describe, not to dazzle. We stress this point because so many physician-witnesses forget their reason for being in court. They make speeches or (if one lends a charitable ear to the performance) deliver monologues. Though these might draw raves at a professional gathering, from the witness box they become merely hot breezes, wafting aimlessly over the jury box before disappearing out the courtroom window, carrying the case with them.

When you testify, look at the lawyer as she puts the question; look at the jury as you answer. Keep your voice up, but do not shout. Speak plainly, using words the jury can understand. Remember, given a choice between accurate medical terminology ("patella") and a familiar equivalent ("kneecap"), take the latter every time. When asked to read from a hospital record, for example, translate as you go along.

When responding to questions, whether during direct examination or on cross, treat your listeners as intelligent people who wish to understand you. If in a particular situa-

tion you think it best to use both the technical word and the plaintext, mention the ordinary word promptly. In time, you will find that you do not need to use the technical word at all. No loss. Remember: The object is to teach the jury, not to demonstrate your medical vocabulary.

Why, we wonder, do doctors have such difficulty grasping and applying this concept? Can it be that, when a physician finds herself in an unfamiliar milieu where the dominant hands belong to someone else, she seeks to reassert control by using a kind of secret language? How ironic. By successfully demonstrating a mastery of the arcane, the doctor-witness renders her message unintelligible. It is as though the teacher deliberately set out to baffle the students.

Although intelligible language is a prerequisite to effective teaching, its use does not alone guarantee the lesson's reception and retention. Like any teacher, you must make your message memorable. How you do so depends on the subject, on your verbal facility, and, in the last analysis, on your imagination. Here, as elsewhere, advance thought and preparation pay off. Never forget the difference between an impromptu performance and one which merely *seems* ad lib.

The apt illustration, presented to the jury as a flash of inspiration, can literally turn the case around. Testifying in a murder prosecution where the defense sought to raise doubts as to the defendant's mental state at the time he admittedly killed the victim, the examining psychiatrist noted that an automobile accident many years earlier had caused a brain injury, which in turn weakened the defendant's ability to control his actions. Medication could mitigate the antisocial effect of the lesion, the physician said. But, the lawyer asked, what would happen without the dosage? "Then," said the psychiatrist, "he would be like a wild horse with the reins cut."

The verdict: not guilty by reason of insanity.

The Witness as Cryptanalyst: Reading Records and Reports

In previous chapters, we have encouraged you to keep in mind the need for plain speech, intelligible to ordinary people (the jurors) ignorant of medical and scientific terminology. We urged you to put your testimony into everyday words, even when you would ordinarily use technical terms to convey your meaning. Although we were then referring to *oral* communication, the principle applies with equal force to medical writing, and perhaps even more strongly to medical *hand*writing.

We are concentrating at this point on two varieties of written matter: the report and the hospital record. Our focus is narrow, because we will deal only with your interpretative function. We leave for later discussion the potential problems inherent in *preparing* a report; and we also defer considering the difficulties likely to beset a witness undergoing a cross-examination based on his own written product, or (worse) on a published article, paper, or treatise of his own authorship.

The framework of inquiry can of course vary. Generally, however, the question arises during that part of the exami-

nation (direct or cross) that probes the basis for the expert's conclusions. Here counsel will want to know what you considered in the course of forming your opinion. Invariably, the hospital record figures prominently at this point. Further, unless you happened to have actually treated the plaintiff (and sometimes even then), the written report of another physician probably also played a part in your thinking.

As in so many other situations, the guiding principle is clarity. If you testify that one of the matters you took into account was Dr. Easy's report, make sure, first, that you state clearly what exact language you had in mind. Do not guess; do not rely upon your memory; do not paraphrase. Instead, put it this way: "I received a copy of Dr. Easy's report, which I have here in front of me. He says: . . ." Read *slowly,* but not with the singsong speech cadence of a bus-terminal announcer, the particular text you considered. If the material is extensive, do not try to recite it all at once. Translate as you go, breaking down the presentation into manageable, understandable bites.

The order we suggest here differs from our proposal about live testimony. There we urged using the ordinary word first, and then—only if necessary—introducing the technical language. If you do that when interpreting a record, you run the risk of veering from the text, with the consequent invitation to objections from the other side. You might, however, consider giving the plaintext first, followed by the actual written language, followed by a repeat of the translation. Do not worry about sounding repetitive. Provided the segments are brief, so as not to confuse the listeners, repetition can be an effective educational tool: "Tell them what you are going to teach; teach; then tell them what you have just taught."

Remember, though, that the subject of your instruction at this point is linguistic, not substantive. You aim to explain, in lay terms, what the report says; you are not trying to evaluate its medical significance. Thus it is entirely proper to say: "Dr. Easy's report says: 'The patient demonstrated crepitus in the third metacarpal joint.' That means he could hear creaking when he moved the patient's finger." It would *not* be appropriate to add, "'That is, Dr. Easy was concerned about arthritic

changes." It would even be improper to say, at this point, "That means the patient probably had some arthritic changes." You may indeed have reached a well-founded opinion on the matter, which you will in due course receive full opportunity to state. Midway through reciting the report, however, is not the right time.

The distinction is really quite simple: Testimonially and logically, the basis for an opinion stands separate from the opinion itself. This principle applies, whatever the format in which the expert proffers the opinion, and regardless of the order in which opinion and basis come into evidence.

Up to now, we have been talking about interpreting a *report*, prepared in connection with litigation or in the course of treatment. The same concepts apply when the document you are analyzing is a hospital *record*. The nature of the record, however, brings the need for additional warnings.

A hospital record contains many sections. In the ordinary case, only some are of any forensic interest: the admitting note or intake sheet; the operation note; the medication sheet; the progress notes; the nurses' notes; and the discharge note or summary. Although others, such as pathology reports, radiology reports, vital-signs records, and routine lab-work reports, can have importance in a particular case, the items we have mentioned are by far the most commonly significant. If you have any opportunity to examine the record before trial—an opportunity you should demand, even if the lawyer who retained you does not suggest it—spend it familiarizing yourself with these essential parts of the chart.

When you come to deal with any part of the record in court, never forget that what you, with a lifetime in medicine, consider commonplace and routine, almost boringly simple, most jurors (and judges) will regard as esoteric and more incomprehensible than encrypted hieroglyphics. You must therefore seize every opportunity not only to translate the data, but to explain the matrix. When asked to read from an operation note, for example, you may properly tell the jury what an operation note is.

Obviously, a certain deftness is very much in order, lest the

opposing lawyer object that "He's lecturing irrelevantly, Your Honor." It is, however, entirely proper to say, as you turn the page, preparatory to answering a question: "I'm looking at the operation note, which is what a surgeon should dictate as soon after the surgery as conveniently possible, describing what took place in the operating room."

Here again, your tone should be instructional, yet not didactic; informal, yet not chatty; colloquial, yet not unscientific. Imagine yourself giving an explanation to an intelligent, eager-to-learn friend. Take the time to go over the material carefully. When the lawyer asks you to read something, do so at reasonable speed, neither tearing through the text nor limping along.

If the material is handwritten, proceed with caution. Make sure of the words. Better to take a moment or two to puzzle out an eccentric calligraphy (even at the risk of emphasizing the obscurity of the writing) than to plunge ahead, with frequent interruptions for self-correction (thus confusing the listeners totally).

As with reports, when you read, you should feel free to insert a definition, or even an explanation, so long as your manner is neither cursory nor condescending. You should not, however, at that stage undertake to explain anything but the words. Your purpose here is merely to ensure that the jurors have a solid basis for understanding the heart of your testimony—your opinion.

The art of interpreting and translating a hospital record receives much less attention than it deserves from both the medical and the legal professions. Properly done, the process serves not only as a necessary underpinning for the witness's opinion, but also as an opportunity for the expert to win the jury's confidence and respect. People generally have positive feelings toward those who lead them through difficulties and toward those who convey the image of openness, of not holding anything back. When you testify, you should put those psychological principles to your own good use.

Different Hypo, Different Needle

Whether we like it or not, whether we regard it as wise or foolish, efficient or wasteful, the legal system has over the centuries devised a format—or, more accurately, a method—for conveying information to the jury. We intend neither to condemn the courts' operating pattern, nor to defend it. Instead, we will try to explain it to you, and to urge that you spend your energy not to fight the system but to make it work for you.

In a perfect world, or even in a medical amphitheater, the most effective teaching arrangement would ask nothing more of an expert witness than that, after stating name and qualifications, she proceed to deliver her opinion in whatever didactic arrangement she believes would be effective and (at least from her standpoint) most comfortable.

The world of law, like life itself, does not attain perfection, or even perfect rationality. Given the courtroom dynamic—namely, the need to put a group of ordinary people (the jurors) in position to decide *factual* issues, the legal framework functions quite well. Indeed, if one understands and accepts its

premises, without necessarily endorsing them, the system offers about as efficient and fair a dispensation as one could reasonably expect imperfect humans to produce.

What distresses physicians, and indeed most witnesses trained to the scientific method, is that the testimonial arrangement ignores almost entirely the mental comfort of the testifying expert. Instead, it focuses entirely upon what is entering into and acting within the minds of the jurors.

The principles are simple:

An expert, once the judge has determined her to be qualified in a particular field of knowledge, may render an opinion in her area of expertise.

At some point, either before or after opining, the witness must disclose the presumed factual basis upon which the opinion rests.

Because only the jury can properly determine the truth or falsity of *any* purported fact, the witness cannot postulate the existence of the essential data. Instead, she must *assume* that the factual predicate is true.

To ensure that everyone—jurors, judge, opponent, and the witness herself—understands precisely what facts the witness is assuming to be true, the question eliciting the opinion must clearly indicate the assumptions which the questioner is asking the witness to make.

In most jurisdictions, the device for creating the requisite clarity is a question specifically inviting the witness to *assume* the truth of the facts which counsel knows—from prior consultation with the witness—form the grounds for the opinion. In some states, however, and in the federal courts, the witness is permitted to give an opinion directly, without the preliminary of a so-called hypothetical question, leaving to the cross-examiner the job of asking the witness to make the assumptions explicit.

Because most physicians find testifying in response to a hypothetical question much more difficult than merely stating a conclusion and then supplying reasons, we will concentrate on suggestions for dealing with the "hypo" and the concomitant "needle."

Typically, an attorney elicits an opinion through some variant of a dialogue like this:

Q. Doctor, I ask you to assume that on October 1, 1986, the plaintiff was a healthy woman of forty-six, weighing 125 pounds, and standing about five feet six inches; that she had no prior history of arthritis or joint disease; that she followed a normal diet-and-exercise program; that she had never suffered injury to the right leg or knee; that on October 1, 1986, the plaintiff was involved in an automobile accident; that at the moment of impact her car was going between thirty and thirty-five miles per hour; that the impact caused her to be thrown forward in such a way that her right knee contacted the dashboard in front of her; that she was immediately taken to the hospital, where X-rays demonstrated a fracture of the proximal third of the tibia; that the fracture line extended into the plateau of the tibia; that the patient was immobilized in a long-leg cast and traction in the hospital for three weeks; that she was [and so on, detailing as much of the patient's history as the lawyer believes is relevant to the case at hand]. Now, Doctor, bearing those assumptions in mind, do you have an opinion, to a reasonable degree of medical certainty, as to whether striking the right knee in the manner I have asked you to assume caused the [symptoms, pain, condition, misalignment—whatever is the pertinent issue]?

A. Yes, I do.

Q. And what is that opinion?

A. The impact of the knee against the dashboard caused the [whatever].

Q. Now, doctor, keeping those same assumptions in mind, do you have an opinion, to a reasonable medical certainty and taking into account advances in medical science to October 1, 1986, as to what medical treatment the average qualified orthopedic surgeon practicing her specialty should have rendered to the plaintiff, under the circumstances I have asked you to assume?

A. Yes, I do.

Q. And what is that opinion?

A. A long-leg plaster cast for about four weeks, or until X-ray demonstrated a good showing of new bone growth along the line of the fracture, followed by [whatever the course of treatment should be].

And so it goes, until the attorney has obtained from the doctor an opinion, "to a reasonable medical certainty," about all the pertinent aspects of the case.

Now, this may seem to you inefficient, not to say silly and unnecessary. As we have said, from your standpoint, or that of anyone used to the scientific, didactic method of instruction, it probably is everything you accuse it of being. In the courtroom, however, the method makes a great deal of sense. Here is why:

The odious hypothetical question ensures that jury, judge, and opposing counsel know exactly what underlies the expert's opinion. If the questioner states a fact not in evidence, the opponent can object, and the judge can decide whether to strike the question or (as is more usual) permit it, subject to an explicit promise by the proponent that future testimony will produce the missing element. If for whatever reason the missing fact does not come into evidence before the end of the trial, the judge will, upon the opposing lawyer's request, order the jury to disregard the entire opinion—or at least so much of it as rested on the now discredited assumption. We say "discredited" because an assumption which lacks an *evidentiary* foundation is, forensically speaking, a false assumption, and thus cannot support a valid opinion.

Failure to provide the evidentiary underpinning can have serious, even fatal consequences. If the opinion is essential to proving the claim, the judge (after an appropriate motion) will dismiss the case. No one can really quarrel with the procedure. If, for example, to establish liability, the plaintiff must persuade the jury that the surgeon failed to meet the standard of the average surgical specialist; and if the only evidence to establish any such failure rests on an assumption

that the surgeon ordered excessive replacement blood; and if the plaintiff's attorney introduces no evidence at all that would permit the jury to conclude that the surgeon gave such an order, then it is entirely fair that the case should end.

The rule that an opinion is no stronger than its underlying assumptions applies, of course, to *any* expert testimony, whether or not the case involves malpractice, and without regard to which side has called the witness. Thus, if a doctor called by the defense, having been asked to assume a prior history of arthritis, concludes that the trauma of the accident did not cause the plaintiff's present arthritic condition, and if by the end of the trial the defense has not introduced any evidence of such a prior history, then the opinion dies.

Laying out the factual basis for the testimony also enables the opponent to cross-examine more efficiently and effectively. When, as frequently happens, the parties do not agree as to one or another of the assumed facts, the opposing lawyer may very well say, for example: "Doctor, in giving your opinion, you were asked to assume that the patient had not been intubated until 3:00 p.m. I ask you to assume instead that he was intubated at 2:15. Would that change make any difference in your opinion?"

Remember, in a courtroom, only the jurors decide the facts—any and all facts. So, if the jury concludes that any assumption is indeed inaccurate, the entire opinion falls, and the jury will give it no weight whatsoever. This is not so dramatic and abrupt an eradication of the opinion as the judge's striking the testimony for lack of evidence supporting one or more assumptions. Nonetheless, if, after hearing the entire case, the jury decides not to credit the assumption—that is, not to believe the assumption to have been valid—the opponent will win, unless the jury has heard *and credited* other evidence making the same point. Because judges generally disfavor duplicative testimony, it is not likely that the trial record will contain any such material.

The transcendent importance of tying the opinion to assumption of facts which the jury *can* find from the evidence makes it essential that you, as an expert, have clearly in mind

the facts you will be assuming or that you will be asked to assume. It is not enough to have reviewed the records and discussed the matter with counsel at an earlier time. It is not enough even to have a firm understanding in your own mind as to the facts supporting each conclusion. You must make certain that the attorney who is calling you as a witness (a) knows every fact which underlies your opinion; and (b) has ensured the presence, *in the record*—i.e., the *trial* record—of each of those facts.

If you are the treating physician, or an examining physician, you have probably previously prepared a written evaluation of the case. Send the attorney—well before trial—another copy, underlining every single fact germane to your conclusions. This pertains especially to the factual matters not contained in the medical materials which you will already have reviewed. The hospital records and medical reports you certainly can competently examine and assimilate. It is the nonmedical facts that offer the prospect of testimonial disaster. If your opinion rests to any degree on one or another version of occurrences, better be sure the evidence is there. If the fracture is consistent with falling from a six-foot height, confirm that the evidence does not disclose a distance of only one foot.

Similarly, if your opinion depends upon medical facts not connected with the present case, learn early whether your understanding is accurate. If you have assumed that the patient has no prior neurological history, do not wait until the trial to learn that she has suffered from migraine since age twelve.

Do not hesitate to put your request in writing. "I am basing my opinion on the facts I have underlined on the enclosed copy of my letter to you dated ————. If you have learned any facts differing from what is contained here, please let me know immediately." Ask, also, for a copy of the answers counsel has filed to the opponent's "expert interrogatories." Required in the federal courts and in most states, these are written detailed synopses of your opinion and the grounds for it. You will find them useful in preparing your testimony. If you discover any difference between the answers and what

you are going to say, tell the lawyer immediately. Opposing counsel will use the discrepancy to embarrass you; if the gap is sufficiently wide, the judge may even exclude your testimony completely. This is not so unfair as it may seem. "Expert interrogatories" and the correlative answers permit the lawyers to prepare intelligent and focused cross-examinations, to avoid testimonial ambush, and thus to reduce the witness's time in court. Most lawyers and experts have no trouble with them. Occasionally, problems can arise. As usual, it is better to learn any bad news early.

If your deposition has been taken, be sure to obtain a copy and to study it thoroughly. Here again, the idea is to avoid surprises and to alert the lawyer who has retained you to any potential trouble spots, particularly any difference between what you said (or opined) then and the opinion you plan to give in the impending trial.

Admittedly, all this amounts to a large investment of time and effort, just to conform to the requirements of a profession you probably do not rank high in your pantheon. Why go to the trouble? The answer is quite simple. In the first place, when you agree to testify, you are committing yourself to perform a task to the best of your ability. The job description includes presenting your evidence in the manner and format most likely to persuade the jury. Our entire discussion has aimed at increasing your persuasiveness.

If the professionalism of doing a job right is not sufficient impetus, we suggest another. When you take the stand, you are to a greater or lesser extent putting at risk your own reputation for accuracy, competency, and truthfulness. *Your* reputation; not the client's; not the lawyer's. Why not use every reasonable technique for preserving and enhancing that reputation? Is not prevention the best and easiest cure?

You Ought to Be in Pictures

Although most expert testimony enters the record in open court, most parties want to learn ahead of trial exactly what the other side's witness will say. Less frequently, a party, anxious to ensure the availability of vital testimony, will seek to record the evidence for future use, thus guaranteeing that, if at the time of trial the witness should be sick, dead, or otherwise unavailable, the jury will nonetheless receive his evidence. In another, rarer, variation, an expert will agree to furnish evidence, but not if doing so entails a court appearance. Whatever the impetus for "canning" the testimony, the device of choice is something you have already encountered, the deposition.

The concepts and techniques we will be discussing in this chapter apply, whichever side has asked you to testify. However, as an independent, nonparty expert—that is, an expert who is not one of the litigants—you will have a different on-camera role depending upon the purpose of the deposition and the side which is conducting it. If the opponent's attorney is at bat, the same considerations pertinent to a party's depo-

sition apply. You might like to reread Chapter Five at this point. Once again, remember, "anything you say can and will be used against you in a court of law."

First of all, the lawyer wants to learn your opinion. Second, he seeks to pin you down—that is, to commit you to a particular theory, so that, bad as it may be from his client's standpoint, it will not turn into anything worse when you come to court. Third, he also wants whatever he can get in the way of ammunition for in-court cross-examination.

Thinking about this, you might conclude that a *discovery* deposition varies only slightly from what you can expect during the trial. Further reflection may show you some significant differences. On the one hand, because the attorney wants to discover how you appraise the case, he may be inclined to give you considerable scope, to make sure you have held out nothing which could produce an unpleasant courtroom surprise. It is just an application of the Herman Hickman Principle which we mentioned in Chapter Four: Don't defer learning the bad news.

On the other hand, the lawyer has to keep in mind the possibility that you will not be available at trial—because of a conflicting engagement, or perhaps illness, or even death. In that eventuality, the attorney who originally retained your services will use the deposition transcript as a substitute for live testimony. Like nondairy creamer, it can never quite replace the real thing; but it certainly beats having nothing.

You see the dilemma: If the lawyer brings out too much of the opposing expert's opinion, he may find his thoroughness haunting him during trial, when the opponent puts the transcript into evidence. If to prevent that possibility he stints his examination, he may give the witness excessive scope for courtroom scrambling. Most experienced lawyers tend to resolve the conflict pragmatically. They reason that having too little knowledge is more dangerous than having too much; and they gamble that the expert's travel schedule, health, and life expectancy will not prevent a live courtroom appearance.

Sometimes the purpose of the deposition, right from the start, is to preserve the expert's testimony, to make certain

that, whatever the vagaries of future events, the proponent will never lack the vital testimony. Here, of course, the emphasis shifts completely. Now it is the party's own witness who is giving evidence. Direct examination, therefore, will aim for the fullest disclosure. The opponent's cross-examination, on the other hand, will press vigorously to destroy the witness, or at least to neutralize his effect.

Because the deposition will take the place of live examination at the trial, and because reading a transcript, even with the most mellifluous inflection, generally carries the excitement of a snail race, many lawyers nowadays conduct this type of examination before a video camera. The product conveys the needed evidence—that is, information—in a form which, thanks to the prevalence of television in our society, jurors find much more familiar, and hence more palatable.

By contrast, you, the expert witness, will find a videotaped deposition not at all like the old-fashioned sort. Still less will it resemble testifying in court. No matter how often in the past you may have submitted to a routine deposition, either at a lawyer's office or your own, your first on-camera experience will jolt you. Likewise, even the veteran of innumerable trips to the witness box will find that testifying by video contrasts with giving evidence in the jury's presence.

Unless you keep the differences firmly in mind at all times, your video testimony will significantly lose effect. The converse, however, is also true. Thus, if you remain thoroughly alert to the nature of the medium, you can actually put the camera to work for you, making your presentation even more effective than the live version.

The first point, although perhaps the most obvious, is one which many novices (and some old hands) forget: The stenographer reports and the tape recorder hears; but the camera sees. Once the video starts to "roll," everything you do will end up on permanent record. *Everything,* including: that unfortunate grimace; the long pause before you answer; the frenzied pawing through records to locate a misplaced paper; those desperate help-beseeching glances toward the attorney.

A videotaped deposition is not a movie. It uses a single

camera, whose position generally remains constant during the exercise. The camera's purpose (and the camera operator's) does not extend to making you look good. The star receives no preparation by way of makeup or rehearsal. If you flub a line, you will receive no second chance. You will have no director to make sure the camera angle flatters you, nor any opportunity for a retake if the first shots do not come out well.

In addition, testifying on video (or even in a conventional deposition, for that matter) raises many of the very same problems that a courtroom appearance does. You still must exercise the same caution in understanding questions; you must answer only what the question asks; you must avoid volunteering material that the question does not cover.

Despite the need for care, a videotaped deposition gives the deponent (that's you, the testifying expert) a distinct edge: the home-field advantage. Although the scene for most ordinary depositions is the office of one or another of the participating lawyers, most (but not all) videos shot to preserve an expert's testimony for trial take place in the witness's office. Thus you can choose your costume, so to speak, and, within limits, the physical setting. You can arrange to appear on camera wearing your familiar white coat, seated at your own desk, with your medical books in the shelf behind you. Apart from giving you the comfortable feeling that everyone gets from performing even an unusual task in friendly surroundings, this setting allows you to present the image of the physician you are, rather than the witness the jury would see and hear if you testified from the stand.

Another advantage is more subtle. Certainly no one will dispute that most people are unaccustomed to receiving important information from a stranger speaking in a courtroom—speaking, indeed, not directly but, rather, through the awkward filter of under-oath question-and-answer. Beyond that, most of us are, in this television age, far more used to learning from the small screen than we are from a live instructor. After all, year-round, most children spend at least as much time in front of television sets as they do in class-

rooms; even the schoolroom depends to a large extent on instructional video of one kind or another. Therefore, when jurors meet a witness, as it were, through a television monitor, they find the format, again, much more familiar than the courtroom experience.

Video, whether from the studio or the office, remains a "cool" medium, which penalizes visual excess. The viewer feels a much greater physical closeness to the on-screen speaker than a juror does to the witness stand. What in court would come across as mere vocal projection appears on video as overbearing insistence. A tone of voice that a courtroom observer would find pleasantly convincing becomes, in the intimacy of the small screen, intolerably arrogant, and hence counterpersuasive.

Manner of speech, vocal cadence, and tonal variety all become critically important. A habit of prefacing each sentence with "Ummmm," annoying enough in the flesh, will drive video watchers mad. Monotony of delivery, never stimulating under the best circumstances, magnifies its soporific effect exponentially when the droning comes out of the image box.

We are not suggesting, any more than we have previously, that you hire an acting coach. You may, however, find it useful, particularly if you have never testified on video before, to suggest that the attorney who has retained you arrange for an abbreviated test run (or screen test, if you prefer to call it that). Some lawyers prefer not to conduct even a brief familiarization exercise. They fear that the other side may learn of it (often by a simple question on cross-examination) and use the information adversely during jury argument.

If you do undertake the test run, your office is an appropriate "studio," with counsel asking you some of the questions he intends to pose during the actual deposition, or even (to avoid the taint of "rehearsal") questions on an independent topic—anything to get *you* talking. It is not necessary to bring in the full panoply of equipment and personnel. A hand-held home vidicam will provide everything you need in the way of revelation. You can then review the tape on a VCR and plan any needed adjustment.

Remember, the idea is not to ensure that you know your

lines. True, a witness, whether in the courtroom or on camera, certainly becomes something of a performer, if not an actor. We are not, however, recommending that you *memorize* anything. On the contrary, we merely suggest that learning the techniques of persuasion which the particular medium requires will make you not only a more effective communicator, and hence a more effective witness, but will, through the psychology of familiarity, put you more at your ease, and thus, in the end, render the whole experience, if not pleasurable, at least tolerable.

CHAPTER TWENTY-FIVE

Cross-Examination Cross-up

The late Seymour P. Edgerton, a wise, shrewd Boston admiralty lawyer, formulated a principle which his young associates used to call Edgerton's Rule for Cross-examining Experts:

Don't.

In other words: Speech may be silver, but silence is golden.

(Once, after listening while one of his crew tried to explain a disastrous cross-examination, "Edge" responded softly, "Well, good judgment comes from experience—after bad judgment gives you the experience.")

Unfortunately, in cases where medical testimony plays any significant role, Edgerton's Rule frequently fails to control counsel's enthusiasm. The reason is not always clear. Sometimes the lawyer perceives the expert's testimony to have had such a damaging effect that at least some effort to neutralize it seems mandatory. Sometimes counsel fears that failure to cross-examine will send the jury a subliminal message of surrender. Sometimes the attorney thinks that giving up on cross-examination will sit poorly with her client. And sometimes, to

be fair about it, an expert is legitimately vulnerable. Perhaps she misstated a fact, ignored pertinent data, or simply exhibited easily demonstrable ignorance (like the physician who testified in a Boston courtroom that the intervertebral discs *surround* the spinal cord). Even Edgerton's Rule has its exceptions.

As the subject of the attention which cross-examination inspires, you will generally be able, after only a few questions, to discern counsel's motive and to handle yourself accordingly. You will use the perceived tenor of the inquiry as the litmus for distinguishing the chef from the short-order cook. Beware the lawyer who approaches the subject tangentially; rejoice at the head-on attack.

The reason is very simple. No matter how inexperienced a witness you are, and no matter how much the lawyer has steeped herself in medical esoterica, the ineluctable fact remains that, in the pertinent field of inquiry, you are a professional and she is not. This does not mean that the lawyer is helpless or that, when the grilling ends, you will certainly step triumphantly from the stand. It does mean that the questioning will all occur in your area of knowledge, not hers.

A second but equally strong reason why the skillful trial lawyer never booms in on a witness—at least not in the initial stages—is psychological. Most jurors, like most people, tend to regard doctors more favorably than they do lawyers. Even more important, as between the witness trying to answer questions, and the hectoring lawyer throwing verbal rabbit punches, most jurors tend to empathize with the victim, rather than the assailant.

The dangerous opponent, from your standpoint, is the quiet one who leads off with, "Doctor, can we agree that . . . ," and who nibbles at the margins of your evidence, trying to obtain a concession that, for example, *if* the chart had shown a lower temperature than what the patient was actually spiking, a different treatment might well have been considered.

This lawyer is hoping that somewhere along the line you will deny that a change in the facts would alter your opinion. That way, long after you have left the courtroom, she can

argue to the jurors that, in evaluating your opinion, they might wish to remember that you, Samuel Goldwyn–style, did not want to be bothered with the facts, because your mind was already made up.

Of course, if like most people you agree that a change in premises requires, at a minimum, reconsidering an opinion based on outdated assumptions, the good lawyer will not give you an opportunity to explain yourself. Instead, she will hope to remind the jury later of your admission that a different temperature would have dictated a different treatment. If the record permits, she will doubtless add that, because the evidence as to temperature did not square with your assumptions, the jury should in fairness disregard your testimony. The success of this strategy depends, naturally enough, on the lawyer's having developed an evidentiary handhold wide enough to let her argue the factual disparity. It also depends on whether or not "your" attorney has been able to repair any of the damage, either on redirect or by bringing in solid evidence to shore up your original assumption.

Why, then, apart from incompetence, do lawyers adopt the raging-bull style of cross-examination? Perhaps the only possible justification is the belief that frontal attack may so unsettle a witness that fear or anger will precipitate loss of control. This in turn may, the antagonist hopes, shake out some contradictory statements that can serve usefully during closing argument.

Whatever the theory's validity, you can easily defuse the bomb. No matter what physical stance or verbal tone the lawyer adopts, answer the question in as even a voice as possible. Take lots of inconspicuous deep breaths (but do not sigh). Keep calm. Try to remember how silly an adult looks when working herself into an angry furor. Do not fight. Make admissions gracefully. Above all, stick to the point: Answer whatever question comes your way; do not venture anything beyond the necessary response.

Boiled down, the technique of successfully undergoing cross-examination comes to this: Be content to survive. By that we mean: Do not succumb to the temptation, however plain the

opportunity, to flatten your tormentor. Your role, after all, is not to win the case single-handed, or even to prevent "your" side from losing. Instead, you are there simply to furnish the maximum amount of information which the lawyer calling you can later (in closing argument) put to good use. Remember, her idea of good use and yours may differ. You, however, must defer to her, if for no other reason than that what may seem a medically irrefutable point may not make forensic sense. Or, to put it plainly, what might justifiably be considered a surefire argument to persuade a medical audience may leave a jury flat, or even antagonistic. Conversely, something which the scientific community would regard as whispering trivia might play a major role in winning the jurors' votes.

Notice, once again, how important it is that you and the lawyer take the time, well in advance of your courtroom appearance, to coordinate the presentation. What we said in Chapter Twenty-one, during the discussion of direct examination, applies at least as strongly to cross-examination. Here it is better to attempt to anticipate *areas* of concern and possible vulnerability, rather than to try predicting the precise questions you will face. This does not mean avoiding detailed preparation. Far from it. Mastering the pertinent facts and, even more important, the related documents will pay handsome dividends. An expert who can without fumbling instantly find *the* nurse's note or *the* medication order conveys an irresistible air of competence, certainty, and persuasion. Few responses impress jurors more than an expert's calmly (but not snidely) directing a floundering cross-examiner with a precise reference to just the page where the needed data appear.

This sort of certainty about the material also gives an expert a solid shield against the cross-examiner's darts. Many lawyers, seduced by the ease of acquiring a new vocabulary, forget that grasping the raw data of a lengthy medical record can be, and usually is, a considerably tougher trick. If your cross-examiner puts a question to you that rests on a false assumption as to some portion of the record, and you realize it before she does, you can confidently frame an answer based

on the *true* contents, leaving her to blunder ahead or back off.

It should be obvious that precision of thought, fact, vocabulary, and expression are absolute necessities when sitting on the cross-examination griddle. A hasty answer gains you nothing, and can cost you heavily. Nonetheless, you must take care lest your understandable and entirely appropriate desire for accuracy cause you to appear timid or evasive. If you fall into the habit of indiscriminately asking counsel to repeat or rephrase virtually every question, the jury may begin to think of you as an Artful Dodger, rather than an Accurate Doctor.

When the question is unclear, or not susceptible to a categorical answer, by all means make your confusion known, while simultaneously identifying its creator. But when a straightforward question seeks readily identifiable information, do not—even though you sense the pitfalls the answer contains—scratch for time by asking, "Could you please repeat the question?" Jurors are shrewd observers. Even if your wording is correct, your body language will give you away. It is difficult for a seat-squirmer to generate an aura of persuasive competence. About the only air she conveys is hot and, like her testimony, transparent and insubstantial.

Whoever first said, "Oh, that mine enemy had written a book!" must have known something about cross-examining experts. If you have written a book, published a paper, or expressed yourself in any other permanent form (a video-taped lecture, for example, or testimony in some other legal proceeding, including a legislative hearing), assume that the other side not only knows about it but will have a copy ready to use at trial, the way the lawyers did in the examples you read in Chapter Eleven.

If the testimony you give from the stand differs in any material way from anything you said or wrote earlier, you will almost certainly be forced to admit the discrepancy, without being given the opportunity for immediate explanation. Any explaining, qualifying, or reconciling will have to come, if at all, during redirect examination. How can you dull the impact? Once again, remember the Hickman Principle.

Long before the trial or deposition, review your own perti-

nent literary and testimonial history. Go over your words with
the present medical situation clearly in mind. If you spot *any-
thing* bearing even remotely on the case, note it and bring it
promptly to the attention of the lawyer who retained you.
Explain the effect of the material on your expected testi-
mony; point out the ways in which the statements do not apply,
or apply in a way different from what the opponent may be
expected to assert.

By doing this, you give "your" lawyer some tactical running
room. She may opt to bring out the conflict early, during direct
examination, affording you a friendly opportunity for full
explanation. After that, even if some doubts still remain, at
least the enemy will lack the advantage that comes from dra-
matic confrontation on cross-examination. Besides, by vol-
untarily conceding the possible weakness early, you may very
well gain stature and credibility in the jurors' eyes.

The same principles apply if you have written a report to
the retaining attorney. Here the problem is more likely to be
omission or misstatement, rather than contradiction. In a fairly
common scenario, the opining physician receives an incom-
plete copy of the hospital record, or a less-than-full set of the
treating physician's office records. If you furnish a written
opinion to "your" attorney based on defective data, you will
be at serious risk in court:

Q. Doctor, you say in your report that my client was in the
hospital three times, is that right?
A. Yes.
Q. Did you know that in fact she was admitted four times?
A. No, I did not.
Q. But you know it now?
A. Yes.

From this point, the questioning can take one of several
turns, any of which will at best cause you discomfort:

Q. Did you know it before you testified?
[Say "Yes" and you will have to explain why you did not
mention it during direct. Say "No" and you will hear:]

Q. Well, does it make any difference in your evaluation?
[Say "Yes" and your opinion weakens. Say "No" and you
will present as, at best, stubborn.]

Apart from having made sure, when you wrote the report
originally, that you specified the data on which you based it,
the only antidote for the difficulty is early coordination between
you and "your" attorney. Before you testify, remind the law-
yer about the possibility that you have not received full infor-
mation. Ask explicitly if the lawyer has learned any new medical
facts which you do not know. If so, have the lawyer make full
disclosure to you, and then tell her frankly how the informa-
tion will affect your evidence. The same tactical considera-
tions which entered into the decision about introducing
damaging evidence from your treatise, paper, or recorded
statements come into play here. Making the best of a bad sit-
uation is better than making it worse.

When the Expert
Brings
Bad News

S ometimes a *testifying* expert knows that, in addition to helpful evidence, he carries information which, if brought out, will badly damage the courtroom position of the party whose attorney has retained his expert services. A variant of this scenario occurs if Expert A, who opined that the defendant-doctor had definitely erred, is unavailable for the trial and his replacement, Expert B, reads the record much less favorably to the plaintiff.

In either case, the situation comes very close to the unhappy obligation physicians must regularly confront in hospital or examining room. When, for example, the X-rays, the lab-work results, and clinical observation combine to leave no other conclusion than that the patient has an inoperable brain tumor, the doctor must break the news. Whatever technique he adopts to cushion the blow, ultimately he cannot avoid telling the patient that recovery is impossible. The truth must come out, and only the doctor can convey the message.

In one way, dealing with the attorney who has retained you is easier than bringing bad news to a patient, a matter which

Dr. Lawrence J. Henderson analyzed acutely in a fragment reprinted in Charles Curtis and Ferris Greenslet's delightful anthology, *The Practical Cogitator*. When communicating with a patient, Dr. Henderson cautioned, you have to consider the possibility that the very process of learning the truth may affect the patient's condition appreciably.

Lawyers, we would like to think, can handle adverse information with professional detachment. In any event, although your disclosure will doubtless influence the way the attorney handles the case, the revelation will not change any of the factual underpinning. What the defendant did cannot be undone. The moving finger writes, and having writ moves on. And if the finger happens to have written in a medical record, any attempt to change the writing, whether by piety, wit, or tears, will only make the ruin more certain. (Incidentally, if a doctor—or anyone else—ever has to change a record entry, the only acceptable method is by running a single line through it, leaving the original writing legible.)

Although in no way do we intend to suggest that your personal moral code is irrelevant to your role as a witness, or to any other aspect of your life, court-oriented or personal, we stress now that, when dealing with the lawyer who brought you into the case, you must deliver all the pertinent facts and all your opinions relating to those facts.

Indeed, as your own common sense will tell you, you should give "pertinent" a definition broad enough to ensure that no significant fact or opinion falls through the litigational cracks. We have mentioned this before, but it bears repeating. Tell the lawyer everything conceivably relevant to the case, especially when the impact is likely to be unfavorable. Leave to him the task of sifting the vital from the peripheral.

Your need to recognize the lawyer's operational control of the case raises a delicate question that we and you ought to address without embarrassment. Like many ordinary citizens, many doctors believe that the generic attorney's work ethic, without regard to any given lawyer's working ethics, requires counsel to do everything and anything that may be necessary to achieve the client's goal, which is to win the lawsuit. People

who believe this assume and expect that in the sort of situation we have been discussing, where the expected testimony will probably reduce the client's (and the lawyer's) chances of winning, the lawyer will, obliquely or directly, ask the witness to trim the evidence, perhaps even to change it—in other words, to lie.

That this image persists may be unfortunate, but it is indisputable. Remember the lawyer portrayed in *The Verdict* by the late James Mason? Another character refers to him as the Prince of Darkness; and he certainly appears to fit the description: suppressing evidence, toying with documents, even planting a "mole" in his opponent's entourage. It does not matter that David Mamet, the scriptwriter, admitted the falsity of these touches (and others), inserted just to keep the story moving. Accurate or contrived, the film encapsulates what a large portion of the public believes to be the way lawyers act on behalf of their clients (and what some lawyers believe to be the way doctors react to their own professional misplays).

Certainly, no one can deny that some attorneys (on both sides of the "versus") falsify evidence, just as some internists prescribe needless drugs, some surgeons operate cavalierly, some accountants "cook" the books, and some journalists write fictitious news stories. The overwhelming majority of lawyers, like the same proportion in other professions, act honestly and ethically. Whether they do so from moral imperative, fear of discovery and disgrace, or a belief that chicanery loses more cases than it wins, the fact remains that, unhappy though a lawyer may be to learn bad news, he will most likely react not by suborning perjury but by planning ways to neutralize the unfavorable impact.

Enter again the Hickman Principle and its close relative, *Primum non nocere*. Recuperative strategies generally revolve around timely disclosure of the unfavorable item. The idea is to bring the information to the jury's attention, but to do so at a moment when and in a manner which will least damage the client's forensic position.

Suppose counsel for a surgeon-defendant has retained you to give an opinion about the doctor's decision to proceed with

a general-anesthetic operation before first ascertaining that the patient was not pregnant. Suppose further that the anesthetic would present serious chemical risks to the fetus, and that a surgeon adhering to normal professional standards would not have gone forward if he knew his patient was pregnant. Suppose that in the operating-room lobby, the surgeon, knowing that the patient and her husband regularly engaged in unprotected intercourse, said, "Are you pregnant?," and the patient (a thirty-six-year-old professor of botany) replied, "No. I wish I were, but I'm certainly not." Finally, assume that neither doctor nor patient said anything further; the operation took place; the patient turned out to have been pregnant; and the fetus spontaneously aborted from the effects of the anesthetic.

You are ready to testify that under the circumstances the surgeon made sufficient inquiry. If the jury accepts your view, it will conclude that the conduct did not amount to malpractice. Going over the case with you a day before trial, the surgeon's attorney says, "With a highly intelligent woman practically swearing she wasn't pregnant, it's hard to think of anything more the doctor could have done." You say: "Well, I suppose he *could* have ordered a pregnancy test. The patient wasn't presenting any kind of emergency, and in a hospital the test result would have been ready within two or three hours."

What can the lawyer do now? As a result of pretrial discovery proceedings, he knows that, although the plaintiff's expert will testify that it was improper to start the anesthesia without a definite, negative pregnancy-test result, the expert has so far been silent on the ready availability of the test.

The first question for the lawyer, therefore, is whether the expert will in fact discuss the point during direct examination. Probably not, he concludes, reasoning that, if the other side has not pressed the matter up to now, it is likely (although not certainly) out of the game plan. Should defense counsel, then, raise the issue himself, on cross-examination? Most trial lawyers would probably give the tactical answer No, because bringing up the fact would only weaken the defendant's case.

The real question is whether the attorney should ask *you* about the test during your own direct examination; he might also consider bringing it out while conducting the defendant physician's direct.

Although you may feel a little queasy that the lawyer should hesitate at all, the problem, while difficult in strategic terms, raises no ethical dilemma. Remember, this piece of evidence (the handiness of the test) is an item independent of the case's factual underpinning. It is, moreover, a matter equally available to each side, through the professional knowledge of their respective experts. Under those circumstances, the defense need not advise the plaintiff of the fact's significance. To paraphrase the late Supreme Court Justice Robert Jackson, nothing requires lawyer-adversaries to share their wits with the other side.

Most probably, defense counsel will decide not to bring out the pregnancy-test point during his direct examination of either you or the defendant, leaving the introduction to come up, if it ever does, when plaintiff's lawyer has you (or the defendant) "on cross." Where does that put you?

More than ever, you must be particularly careful about your responses. Most important, you do not want to bring out the delicate matter inadvertently. Make sure that you understand each question, and that your answer does not exceed the bounds of the inquiry. Thus, for instance, if the plaintiff's attorney asks, "The defendant did not obtain the results of a pregnancy test, did he?," your answer is properly "No." Anything more than that may lead to additional questioning, which may in turn take matters who knows where. We repeat our prior advice: On cross-examination, the less a witness says (while adequately answering all questions), the better.

Of course, if at any time, either as a follow-up to your "No" or in some other part of the cross, the lawyer asks about the in-hospital availability of the pregnancy test, and how long getting a result would normally take, you *must* answer truthfully. Nothing, however, requires you to show surprise, shock, embarrassment, or dismay. Once again, the idea is to make certain you understand the exact question and to give the

minimum response. Speak clearly, matter-of-factly, and in your normal tone of voice.

Unfortunately, counsel may very well pursue the subject. You might expect something like, "And so far as you can tell, the record shows no reason why the defendant could not have waited the two or three hours necessary to obtain a definitive test answer?" The only acceptable answer, in terms of the truth, your credibility with the jury, and common sense, is, "That is correct."

Avoid the understandable temptation to lessen the damage. It cannot be done; and the effort will probably worsen the situation. Any spin control should come from defendant's counsel, during redirect examination. He is, after all, better positioned than you to assess the trial, and certainly better trained in repair techniques.

The example we have dissected concerned a defense expert. Here is a comparable situation involving a plaintiff's witness:

An orthopedic surgeon, retained to testify to the failure of the defendant to meet professional standards, learns from a careful reading of the hospital record that the patient several times refused medication. Although that has nothing to do with the *liability* aspect of the case, it does pertain to the issue of damages for pain and suffering. What should the doctor do? The answer on this side of the "versus" exactly parallels what we said about the defendant's expert, because the testimonial and moral issues are adversarially neutral, and thus liable to confront any litigant—and any expert witness.

One final situation, fortunately rare, is worth discussing. Suppose after your initial review of the record (which for present purposes we can assume to be complete) you conclude that any opinion you can give will directly counter the position of the lawyer who wishes to retain you. The attorney then pays you for your time and says he will no longer need your services. Or suppose that, after you have pointed out a bit of adverse evidence, like the pregnancy-test and medication-refusal situations, the lawyer similarly terminates your relationship. What, if any, responsibilities do you have at that point?

You face three possibilities:

- Do nothing.
- Wait for the other side's attorney to contact you, then disclose to him what you have concluded, and why.
- Bring your information voluntarily to the opposing lawyer.

Although, like most ethical dilemmas, this one raises doubts, you would probably deal with the matter least unsatisfactorily by doing nothing. Any other alternative puts you in a difficult moral position. When you first agreed to consult, your signing on carried with it, at the very least, an obligation not to betray the interests of the side retaining you. In most states, that would probably be a *legal* as well as an *ethical* restraint.

Thus going to the other lawyer with your information is not a viable option, neither is some form of "hinting" communication. If the lawyer comes to you, you ought to decline employment, because if you go over to the former enemy you will find yourself in an inescapable conflict. Your continuing duty to your former affiliation requires you to keep silent; your new employer will properly expect you to bring to his attention any matter useful to his client's case. In any event, here, too, "hints" are out.

Remember, you are not obliged or expected to approve the acts or omissions of the original lawyer-retainer. Neither, however, are you morally or legally required to police *his* ethics. If one of these posers arises, or if the less difficult bearer-of-bad-tidings case confronts you, just remind yourself that, although you may be the unwilling agent of difficulty, you did not make the facts. You are in no way responsible for ameliorating their moral effect, or for resolving any ethical conundrum they may produce.

Consultation:
A Different Opinion

Some doctors barely tolerate participating in court proceedings, whether as litigant, witness, or even spectator. A few (although more than most physicians care to admit) positively enjoy the experience. The largest segment of the medical profession, however, like the majority of people in all walks of life, rank testifying as a top contender for the activity-most-to-be-avoided. Chances are, this majority includes you.

At the same time, you may, through inclination or duty, feel disposed to participate, provided you can do so without inconvenience, pain, or embarrassment. Perhaps you believe that a physician should assist in exposing unquestionably substandard medicine. Conversely, maybe you feel that a doctor should come to the aid of a fellow professional caught unfairly in a firestorm of criticism. Whether from one of these motives, or even some impetus slightly less noble, you remain willing to play a role, so long as it calls for no onstage appearance, not even a silent walk-on.

This, we can assure you, is not only entirely appropriate, but highly useful to a litigating attorney. The reason is sim-

ple. Many doctors not only dislike the legal system but actively try to remain uninvolved with it, if involvement means even the *possibility* of a court appearance, with all the time-consuming, schedule-shredding discomfort that the average physician quite accurately equates with courthouse activity. We want to talk about associating yourself with the *medical* aspects of a lawsuit while avoiding any contact with the court itself.

Frequently, when an attorney approaches a physician to discuss medical concerns, the doctor's antipathy to taking the witness stand makes the interview tense and unproductive. If the doctor's aim is to stay out of court, while the lawyer's is to find out *and bring into the trial* as much helpful evidence as possible, the two professionals fall into a hopeless clash of interests.

The more the lawyer gleans information which, she believes, will enable the client to obtain a successful courtroom result, the more she will want the doctor to testify. This eagerness will communicate itself to the doctor through the lawyer's tone of voice, body language, and general demeanor. Even an inordinately unperceptive physician will soon realize that the surest way to end up on the witness stand is to give the lawyer useful medical ammunition. Thus the doctor carefully restrains any tendency toward helpfulness.

Certainly, a lawyer would prefer to have both the useful information and an eager-to-testify physician. At least in the earlier stages of the case, however, she will settle for the information. Having it cannot harm her case; and it will most probably enable her to understand the medical issues better and thus to achieve greater rapport with whatever other physician she may ultimately have to retain. Human nature carrying as it does such a large component of hope, she may also be harboring the fantasy that she will not have to look elsewhere, because eventually, after you have come to know her and to understand how much she and her client need you, you will change your mind and agree to testify, after all.

Whatever counsel's motive, you *can* control the degree of your participation, provided you establish the limits the very

first time you and the attorney confer. It is really quite simple. You have only to say something like this: "I am happy to consult with you. I will not, however, undertake any examination or test of your client, Ms. ———. My fee will be $——— per hour, whether the consultation takes place in person or by telephone; that rate will also apply to any time I may spend reviewing any document whatsoever, and to any time I may spend examining pertinent medical literature. Under no circumstances will I testify for you or your client, either in court or on deposition. Moreover, if anyone else seeks to obtain my deposition or in-court testimony, I will decline; and if I receive a summons for either type of testimony, I will expect you to take, at no expense to me, whatever steps you can to quash the subpoena. If these conditions are acceptable, I will ask you, before we confer, to sign a letter listing them."

In fact, it is not at all out of line to have all this itemized in letter form. When you meet counsel for the first time, give her the letter, in duplicate, after signing both copies. Ask her to sign one, and then keep it in your file.

Does this seem exceptionally stiff and stilted? In a sense, it is. If you feel comfortable enough with counsel's oral assurance that she will never ask you to testify, skip the rest of the formalities. If, however, you prefer to put your relationship on a businesslike basis, experience shows that a written, acknowledged summary of the understanding certainly does minimize the possibility of subsequent unhappiness. Above all, do not feel embarrassed: Western civilization has long recognized the desirability of safety over sorrow, and the consequent value of a written agreement in assuring that safety predominates.

One caveat. The lawyer can only commit herself and her client. She cannot control what the other side may do. She can resist any effort to pull you into an active role, but she cannot assure success. Indeed, if a lawyer insists that under no circumstances will you ever come closer to the case than whatever limits she has promised you, watch out—and ask for specifics. The truth is that you can guarantee yourself immu-

nity from contact with the court only by declining contact with the case and with the lawyer. The choice, we repeat, is entirely yours.

If you do decide to maintain a consultational relationship with a litigating attorney, what is she likely to ask of you? Almost certainly, your first task will involve reviewing the patient's record and the reports of any examining physicians. If the lawyer represents the plaintiff, you can expect a fuller array of information, not because the plaintiff's lawyer deliberately holds anything back from the other side, but because, unless an opponent *asks* for a given item or the judge has ordered its production, the lawyer does not have to turn it over, even if (as is usually so) the lawyer's file contains information which the other side might find interesting.

If either side has conducted the deposition of anyone whose testimony bears on the medical issues, the attorney will probably ask you to review it. Do not hesitate to suggest reading this material, even if counsel does not raise the point on her own. In fact, you should feel free to call her attention to *any* item whose perusal you think might be beneficial.

We are not, of course, proposing that you take the lead in the enterprise, still less that you convey any idea that you are seeking to aggrandize your role (and concomitantly increase your fee). Still, you *are* the expert; your expertise supplies the very reason—the only reason—for asking you into the case at all. If you withhold any suggestion that, in your judgment, has medical importance, you are not rendering the service for which counsel retained you. The considerations raised in the last chapter apply here as well.

You can resolve many potential snarls by developing a basic list of items which you would normally expect counsel to furnish: hospital records; radiology and pathology reports; reports of treating and examining physicians; deposition transcripts; answers to interrogatories; and (in a malpractice case in which you are retained to advise defense counsel) any correspondence between counsel and the defendant physician. Showing these items to you does not destroy the attorney-client privilege, because the privilege covers consultations ancillary

to litigation. That is, disclosure to you does not amount to waiving the client's right to maintain confidentiality.

If you have difficulty with this part of your job or, indeed, any aspect of your interaction with the attorney, do not guess; do not let the question pass. Frankness in these matters, as in the entire relationship, is absolutely essential.

As a "consulting," or teaching, expert, you, unlike the "testifying" expert, can ordinarily (but, as we have indicated, not invariably) anticipate complete avoidance of the courthouse and any offices other than those of the lawyer who is consulting you. Nonetheless, in an occasional case involving particularly difficult technical issues, counsel may ask you to sit with her while she conducts the deposition of one or another witness, lay or medical. You will serve as a combination adviser-interpreter, charged with helping counsel ask the right questions.

This does not occur, we emphasize, in every case. Virtually by definition, the need for your on-site presence arises only when the deponent's evidence would normally tend to favor the opponent. Usually, not unless the attorney expects to cross-examine a witness will she be likely to need you there. When the witness is "friendly," as, for example, a physician whose deposition counsel is taking for future use at trial, the attorney will almost certainly obtain whatever input she wants from you *before* going into battle.

One last thought about you and the consultant's role. If you are interested in the legal system's treatment of medical evidence, and would like to play some part in ensuring that the courts obtain accurate and complete information, advising lawyers may offer you a chance. Beyond that, if you think you might, at some future time, find yourself willing to participate actively, consulting offers a way to scout the territory.

Discharge Summary

Whether you came to this book as a prospective or actual defendant, or in the relatively detached role of expert witness, your reading has, we hope, heightened your awareness of the pitfalls and problems confronting anyone caught up in the legal process.

Beyond pointing out the hazards, we have also tried to indicate the reasons underlying a morass of procedures and principles, concepts which a stranger, particularly a medically trained stranger, would certainly regard as illogical, unfair barbarities. By providing a reliable road map and a list of the significant sights, we have sought to make the bizarre and hostile seem, if not commonplace and friendly, at least understandable and surmountable.

No single book can serve as a complete wilderness guide, just as no one medical treatise can turn a college senior into a physician. After reading what we have written, you will certainly have questions about matters we have not covered in sufficient detail, or indeed not covered at all. Do not hesitate to bring your concerns and your inquiries to the professional

most likely to give you definitive situational answers: the attorney who represents you or who has asked you to assist him as either a consultant or a courtroom witness.

It may well be that "your" lawyer disagrees with one or another position we have taken. As professionals, we welcome second opinions; you, as the object of the advice, may feel slightly less comfortable about having to confront still another congeries of doubts. You might therefore wish to remember that, as Justice Holmes used to say, "Life is not doing a sum; it is painting a picture." So, too, with the physician and the courts.

We look, therefore, at any differences in value, viewpoint, and strategy as normal, healthy, and exceptionally useful. If this book has answered many of your questions, fine. We will, however, rest content if reading it has done nothing beyond stimulating your productive inquiry.

Perhaps we can best sum up thus: A physician into whose life litigation comes is like a patient with an acute, unpleasant, yet survivable disease. We have not sought to offer a cure, because none exists. Instead, we have tried to help you minimize your discomfort and to pass the crisis without serious, deleterious, or permanent after-effects. Everything else, we and you must leave to time, the greatest of all physicians.

Index

expert testimony, *see* testimony of
 expert physicians
expert witness(es), 132–35, 136–39
 clothing of, 158, 174
 credibility of, 133, 134, 135
 definition of, 78
 and diverse backgrounds of jurors,
 154
 effectiveness of, 135
 fees paid to, 135, 140–44, 189
 function of, 135, 146–47
 judge and, 78, 132, 133, 134, 146
 jury and, 132, 133, 134, 136, 137,
 145–47, 153–54, 155, 165, 180,
 181, 182
 lawyers and, 133, 141–42, 156–58,
 169–70, 172, 177–79, 189–90
 layperson's conception of, 135, 136,
 139, 142, 143
 as paid for time and expertise, not
 opinion, 135, 140–41
 required vs. unneeded, 132, 145–46
 as teacher, 134–35, 145–52, 153–59,
 164
 see also testimony of expert physi-
 cian; witnesses
exposure, 100, 101

facial expressions, 66, 67, 70, 72, 80,
 108–9
 videotape and, 173
facts, factual research, 22, 23, 24–25,
 26, 168, 169, 188
 as basis for expert testimony, 169–
 70, 172
 deposition and, 30, 32, 36
 judge's instructions and, 58
 lawyer's preparation and, 24
 see also discovery; evidence
fair result of dispute, 22–23, 26
family, at trial, 67
fear, 6, 8, 17–18, 48
 cross-examination and, 179
federal courts of appeals, 119, 120
fees:
 contingent, 15–16
 of expert witnesses, 135, 140–44, 189
 of jurors, 51
 of lawyers, 3, 8, 11, 15–16

"first impression," 58, 121
foreign words, used in testimony, 150
foreperson, 52, 61, 113
friends, at trial, 67

Goldwyn, Robert, 6
grammar, in testimony, 151
Greenslet, Ferris, 185

Hand, Learned, xi
health-care plan, of plaintiff, 101
hearsay, 95, 115
 appeals and, 42
 in deposition, 32, 36
 exceptions to exclusion of, 42
Henderson, Lawrence, J., 185
Hickman, Herman, 27
Hickman Principle, 27, 172, 181, 186
Highet, Gilbert, 146
Holmes, Oliver Wendell, Jr., 41, 197
hospital records, *see* records and reports
hung juries, 60, 112
hypothetical questions, 165–67

imagination, in testimony, 159
impeachment of witness, 36
inferences, drawing of, 132
information:
 collection of, 24–25, 26: *see also* dis-
 covery
 withholding of, 29
 see also facts, factual research
insurance:
 of plaintiff, 101
 see also malpractice insurance and
 insurers
interrogatories, 13, 26, 28–29
 expert, 169–70
investigative procedures, *see* discovery

Jackson, Robert, 188
jargon, medical, 6, 85, 149–51, 158,
 159, 160, 161
Johnson, Samuel, 25
judge(s), 5, 65–66
 appellate courts' review of, 41, 42–
 43, 59–60, 61, 109–10, 117, 119,
 120–21
 as audience, 63–64

large claims and, 11
lawyers selected by, 8–9, 11
noncooperation claimed by, 10
settlement and, *see* settlement
malpractice litigation:
as applied history, 44
burden of proof in, 83, 107
conflicting recollections in, 40
cost of priority in, 100
doctor's lack of control in, 6, 13, 17,
 63, 68
escalation in, 15–16, 39
fair result in, 22–23, 26
federal courts and, 51–52
necessity of, as system, 15–16
negligence proved in, *see* negligence
obsession with past events fostered
 by, 44–45
plaintiff's claims in, 82–83
prevention of, *see* prophylaxis
prior performance and, 23–24
screening system in, 16–17, 19–20,
 39–40
settlement in, *see* settlement
statistics on outcomes of, 16, 37, 100
see also trial
Mamet, David, 186
medical language, 6, 85, 149–51, 158,
 159, 160, 161
medical science, uncertainties in, 136–
 37
mid-trial settlement, 46, 97–104
right moment for, 98–100
see also settlement
mistrials, 54
monetary compensation, 23, 41
see also settlement
moral issues:
adverse evidence and, 189–90
in defending bad position, 25
and public perception of lawyers'
 work, 185–86
Morrill, Alan E., 53
"mouthpiece," 96

National Practitioner Data Bank
 (NPDB), 46–47, 103–4
negligence, 100
definition, 23–24

and patient's prior condition, 102
and patient's response to medica-
 tion, 101–2
see also malpractice litigation
notebook, in trial preparation, 12–14
discovery and, 27

oath, 32, 36, 53
objections, 54
appellate court review of, 42
in deposition, 31–32, 35
juror view of, 86
off-the-record remarks, 71
"one," used as personal pronoun, 151
opening statements, 52–53, 69–70, 82,
 83
organization, in trial preparation, 12–
 14

Pascal, Blaise, 100
patient, *see* doctor-patient relation-
 ship; plaintiff
"peremptories," 50
perjury, 5, 32, 186
personal impressions, 64
personality, importance of, 92
philosophy, legal, 3, 4
physicians, *see* doctors
plaintiff:
burden of proof and, 83, 107
defense strategy and, 82–83
idiosyncratic response of, 101–2
insurance or health-care plan of, 101
monetary compensation to, 23, 41;
 see also settlement
prior conditions of, 102
see also specific aspects of litigation
post-trial motions, 114, 116
Practical Cogitator, The (Curtis and
 Greenslet, eds.), 185
primum non nocere principle, 17, 73, 91,
 128, 144, 186
proof, burden of, 83, 107
prophylaxis, 122–28
carelessness and, 123
doctor-patient relationship and, 123–
 25, 127
and doctor's supposed infallibility,
 125

television, 174–75
tension and anxiety, 6–7, 9, 12, 41, 45,
 48, 62–63, 65, 112
testimony, 53–57, 76–81
 coaching of, 31
 in direct examination, 157–58, 173,
 187–88
 discredited assumptions in, 167–69
 duplicative, 168
 function of, 131–32
 lawyer's assessment of strengths and
 weaknesses in, 30, 32–33
 objectives of, 76–77, 79
 order of, 53
 see also cross-examination
testimony of defendant-physician, 70–
 75, 83–92
 answering questions in, see questions
 awareness needed in, 71
 body language in, 64, 71–72, 80
 court record and, 70–71
 evidence vs., 71–72
 facial expressions and, 66, 67, 70, 72,
 80, 108–9
 KISS (Keep It Short and Simple), 85
 professional expertise exhibited in,
 84–85
 and textbooks cited in cross-exami-
 nation, 87–91
 and understanding of proceedings,
 73
testimony of expert physician, 129–95
 and attention span of jurors, 155
 and brief exposure to plaintiff, 143–
 44
 case preparation and, 141, 144
 certainty conveyed in, 180–81
 clarity in, 155
 communication and understanding
 in, 147–52, 153, 154–55, 158–
 59, 161, 163
 and communications with opposing
 lawyer, 190
 competence conveyed in, 181
 comprehension in, 155
 conciseness in, 154–55
 consultation as alternative to, 191–
 95

in cross-examination, 21, 133, 140,
 157, 168, 172, 173, 175, 177–83,
 187, 188
against defendant-physician, 18, 19,
 20–21, 39–40, 77–81
for defendant-physician, 83–84
in deposition, 171–76
deposition transcript as substitute for,
 172–73
in direct examination, 157–58, 173,
 187–88
discredited assumptions in, 167–69
factual basis of, 169–70, 172
fees and, 135, 140–41
and frequency of court appear-
 ances, 142–43
hypothetical question in, 165–67
"impromptu" remarks in, 159
and information damaging to law-
 yer's client, 184–90
KISS (Keep It Short and Simple), 85
lack of "feedback" and, 154
language used in, 149–51, 153, 158–
 59, 160, 161
lawyer's strategy and, 141–42
lawyer's termination of relationship
 and, 189–90
lawyer's trial preparation and, 156–
 58
legal process and, 164–70
legal rules on allowance of, 145–46
looking at lawyer and jury in, 158
mandatory vs. exclusory, 145–46
new information and, 183
preparation for, 169–70, 180, 181–
 82
published works used against, 181–
 82
qualification of, 132, 134
on reasoning process leading to
 opinion, 141–42, 144, 161–62,
 165–70
recording of, 171
records and reports in, 160–63
rehearsal of, 157–58, 159
tape used in practice of, 147–48
on video, 173–76
see also expert witness